So, Maurice has joined up with Murdo[...] happened before . . . . way back in 19[...] ready to flourish anew after the war a c[...] decided . . . but read on for yourself. [...] again! Do I need to say more?

John D. Vose.

This book is dedicated to success to all clubs whether Super League or not, and to the great game of Rugby League – long may it flourish!

Acknowledgements

My thanks are due to my son Colin Vose who couldn't stop talking when I mentioned the idea of a book about the Super League! Many of his suggestions are in the book. Also, to my good friend Martin Lloyd, who lifted me when I felt I couldn't write another 'Joshua saga'. On a trip to Ireland the ideas came flooding to our fertile minds in such a stream that we had to stop the car to get paper and pens! To Mike Comber for the typing and to Brian Parkinson for the illustrations. To Maurice Lindsay for giving me the idea!

JOHN D. VOSE

The author wishes to state that all the characters in this book are fictitious and are not based on any person living or dead.

Certainly no disparagement is meant to the old U.C.P. restaurants which graced northern towns for many years selling popular food such as tripe, trotters and other succulent dishes beloved by Northern folk at the time. Sadly such establishments have departed and are replaced by 'fast food' shops which, it must be admitted, appeal to young people. Times have changed!

Neither is the book meant to demean in any way the new Super League or anyone connected in its creation.

John D. Vose

Two other rugby league sagas by John Vose are still available:

UP T' ROVERS! I.S.B.N. 0 9501036 4 0

Joshua Hepplethwaite sets out to save the Rovers from extinction despite the opposition of the local town council.
'As northern as pie and peas!'

PUT REF. A JERSEY ON! I.S.B.N. 0 9501036 5 9

Joshua signs a 'cracking' Welsh stand-off with a drink problem!

Both books are available from all W.H. Smith and Waterstone Branches as well as all booksellers.

SHELLAC PUBLICATIONS

Chapter I

Joshua Parkinson Hepplethwaite, mill owner and chairman of Bramfield Rovers Rugby League Club, was a happy man once again. After the hostilities of the Second World War, rugby league was once more to start up again as a full league. Just as it had been prior to the war.

His team had struggled on during those war torn years when three of his players had been killed in action and others were too war weary ever to play again.

Every week Joshua had fielded a team and at times he wasn't opposed to press ganging likely lads to make up the thirteen. He often laughed to himself at the time he had been called to the turnstile at Central Park. His scrum half, Joe Bott, had been refused admission to the club house because the gate man wouldn't believe he was a player. Joe was sixteen and one of a handful of R.A.F. cadets who helped the Rovers out when they were short of players, which was usually every weekend. He often laughed about the state of the playing field as well.

At the outset of the war old Tom Crook, a local farmer, had asked the club committee if he could graze his cows on the pitch. The fifteen shillings a week rent he offered was too good to refuse and what was just as welcome Joshua and his co-directors, the Keasley brothers, got milk and fresh eggs for "nowt" into the bargain. Call it Black Market if you like but it was common practice in those days. It was a case of if you knew someone "in the know" you could be lucky enough to get food that was rationed. Many a person was sent to jail when caught.

"By gum, we had some fun" mused Joshua as he waited in the parlour for his wife, Phoebe Maud, to powder her nose. At one

3

The dilapidated ground in wartime. Bramfield circa 1942

point in his thoughtful reminiscences he burst out laughing aloud.

"What's funny, love?" called out his wife.

"Ee... I were just cogitating about war, love. I were thinking about that time the groundsman hadn't cleared away all the cow muck ont' Saturday proper. We were playing Saints and their centre, Stanley Powell, shot through a gap in our defence and was going in under the posts when he slips in a dollop! We'd have lost only for that and I had to buy old Tommy Crook the farmer a pint of mild in payment, so to speak."

"They were bad days, Josh love; and yet they were good days" said Phoebe Maud who was now resplendent in her new hat ready to go out with her husband. Joshua had promised her a "reet good treat", a celebration tuck-in at the local U.C.P. restaurant and she was licking her lips in anticipation. Nowt fancy, just good wholesome Lancashire grub: cow heels, trotters and mash. The celebration was because of the happy news that the Rugby League would be resuming once again in autumn. The year was 1945.

The treat was going down well and Joshua was wiping the tripe juice from his corpulent chins when a small, dapper man at the next table gave him a wink. Now Joshua was a no nonsense sort of Lancashire chap who'd heard all about little chaps who winked at well built fellows.

"What does want, lad ?" he enquired testily.

"Am I correct in thinking you are Joshua Hepplethwaite, Chairman of Bramfield Rovers, and this is your good lady ?"

"What if you are, lad ?"

"My name is Seth Scragbottom, Managing Director of United Cattle Products, and I'm pleased to make your acquaintance." He rose to his feet and bowed to Phoebe Maud. Joshua was flummoxed. With a name like Scragbottom, there could be no denying the man's Northern roots, but the bowing and the posh way he spoke wasn't usual for Bramfield.

"And I'm pleased to meet you, too" said Joshua. "So you're the captain of the tripe game, eh? Well it makes me reet proud to meet you. I've already met Harry Ramsden and now you. Two tycoons of gradeley Northern grub, although Ramsden is Yorkshire which spoils it a bit but I reckon as someone has to be born there. You are a Lancastrian I presume?"

"Decidedly, Rochdale. Next street to Gracie Fields in fact, but I've travelled extensively and seen a bit of the world, domiciled in France before the war for a while. I like the way of life there, but I still enjoy a good plateful of my own produce. The meal is on me, by the way".

"Nay lad, I always pays me way".

"I insist. You see our meeting is providential. I have been on the point of approaching a well known rugby league personality and wasn't sure which man to seek out. I had thought of Hadfield Barnacre of Bruddersby Stanley...."

Joshua guffawed an interruption.

"What, that oily toad! He's a bad advert for the game is Barnacre." Unknowingly Mr. Scragbottom had hit a raw nerve. Hepplethwaite and Barnacre were like chalk and cheese in rugby circles. In a sentence they detested each other. Lancashire's Bramfield and Yorkshire's Bruddersby were deadly rivals on the field of play.

"He can't lie straight in bed, that lad. He's as crooked as a corkscrew. But what do you want to talk about ? Am I to take it you're a rugby league fan ?"

"Oh no, Mr. Hepplethwaite. Despite being born within shouting distance of the Hornets ground I must admit that such a rough game has never appealed to me. As you can see from my slight build I was never meant for sporting arenas, certainly not ones in which rugby league is played. Yet I have a deep interest in the future of the sport. Contradictory? Yes." He waved over a waitress in her smart pinny and matching hat.

"Mabel, my dear, will you bring us a pot of tea and I do believe you have some chocolate biscuits saved for a rainy day in the back room ? Thank you, my dear."

"Chocolate biscuits! Well, I never!" exclaimed Mrs. H.

Phoebe Maud was gazing at Mr. Scragbottom as if he was some sort of magician. "Ee, love, it must be 1940, five year ago, when I had one of them. Kardomah, in the Old Shambles, Manchester. I've never seen one since."

"Keep your voice down, love" admonished Joshua. "Careless talk costs lives. Think on. Walls have ears."

"The war's over, Joshua".

"Only just, love and we've still got ration books, dried eggs, carrot jam and soap coupons. Think on."

Just then the waitress placed a plate of succulent chocolate biscuits in the centre of the table. "Get thee behind me, Satan! I don't know where you got 'em from, Mr. Scragbottom, but I'm not bothered. Get stuck in, Phoebe, lass. It's Christmas!" Mr. Scragbottom gave a wry smile.

"A product of France. One of my contacts is a biscuit manufacturer – shall we say he pushed a box into my case when I wasn't looking – ha! ha! As you know, things were dreadful over there as well. But lets look on the bright side shall we? France and England will both be great again and I hope to play a part, however small, in that plan of rebuilding."

"I don't follow you, lad" said Joshua with his mouth full of biscuits. What's he up to? He's a wily one is this lad – you don't get chocolate biscuits for nowt, not these days.

The tripe king's moustache twitched like a sensitive antenna as he poured the tea and his beady eyes glowed in such a manner that reminded Joshua of a Machiavellian characterisation performed by Mr. Bransby Williams, the music hall thespian, at Bramfield Hippodrome back in the twenties. He couldn't make the bloke out. He was an odd un, that was for sure. Why the hell did he want to talk to a rugby league man? Seth could read Joshua's mind.

"I think I better put my cards on the table, Mr. Hepplethwaite, as I believe you are somewhat bewildered why a man who has no love for the game of rugby league should wish to discuss it with

Mr and Mrs Hepplethwaite in the U.C.P.

8

you. But like all good stories do, I will commence at the beginning."

He took a mouthful of tea, adjusted his plus-fours, and began the following story:

"For three years from the start of the war I was an Intelligence Officer stationed in France. I had many adventures but they are all behind me. My counterpart was one Jaques Chevalier, who worked for the French Intelligence. . . . "

"Ee, same name as the singer. . . . I've got some of his records" enthused Phoebe Maud. "They're on that label with t' dog on".

'Every little breeze seems to whisper Louise . . . Birds in the trees seem to whisper Louise . . . I love you Louise!'

"We've got lots of his records haven't we Josh?"

"Aye, but French singers don't go down in Bramfield. I'm a George Formby man meself", remarked her husband.

"Quite" said the tripe king, with just a tiny hint of annoyance at the interruption.

"Jaques and I became firm friends. It turned out that he was a celebrated onion grower from Northern France, the most famous in the whole country. When it became known what my business was, naturally we were referred to as tripe and onions. Although this was a joke at the time, gradually an amazing idea took shape from the whimsical seeds scattered on fertile imaginations. Jaques is an ex rugby league fullback – is that the chappie that stands at the back under the goal posts?"

"You're thinking of soacy – football ", prompted Joshua. "Cissie's game".

"Oh no, he was a rugby league player, built like – what shall I say?"

"A W.C. door ?" suggested Joshua, with a wink. "I'd put it more bluntly if I were on me tod".

"Quite so" laughed Seth. "A large man with a gargantuan love of the game. He couldn't understand why I didn't have the same passion for rugby as he did. He knew about Rochdale and all the other strongholds – St. Helens, Bramley, Hunslet – he was fascinated

9

by the names and the traditions of the clubs who had started the game in England. He is also a visionary. Through some of the darkest hours during the war he would tell me of his dream. He said that one day the English League would amalgamate with the French League to form a Super League. In fact he firmly believes the time will come when Europe will be a close united family. Like one huge country".

"Sounds like a typical Froggie to me, all wind and water. It's ruddy daft talk is that. I've never heard 'owt so silly". Joshua guffawed at the idea. "Yon mon must be bonkers".

"At first I was of your way of thinking, Mr. Hepplethwaite, but when Jaques went into details of his scheme I began to listen, especially when he told me how it was to benefit the tripe industry in this country. He wants to move in to England and become the biggest supplier of french onions to the tripe industry – a reciprocal arrangement."

"What the hell's this got to do with rugby league? It's a load o' tripe that's for sure". Joshua was losing patience. Was this some kind of a joke? If it was it wasn't funny.

"Jaques' idea is to give sponsorship to a revolutionary new league, to pour much needed money into the clubs to enable them to improve the grounds, to create new facilities. He's a very rich man and so am I. Although I've made a lot of money out of my cattle products I am still a relatively young man and want to spread my Northern business all over Europe. Already I have branches in Southern England and one in London. France will follow – the combination of tripe and onions will become a reality on a huge scale never known before.

"Jaques, as I said, is a man of vision and his feet are firmly on the ground. He thinks that the name of the new league should be the U.C.P. Super League as the name means so much in the rugby league strongholds of the north and where, after all, it is very firmly entrenched. League is popular in France, too, but not on the same scale, although he is sure that the code will spread when his Super

League gets going. Of course much thought has gone into the machinations of the running of such a league. He has made a list of stipulations. He has stated the benefits and the rules for the clubs to follow. There will be many radical changes but the benefits to the clubs will be enormous..."

"Aye, and you'll make a fortune out of your tripe and the Frenchman out of his onions and then beggar off and leave us high and dry – I don't like it, Joshua". Phoebe Maud's unexpected outburst rattled her husband who was not used to hearing her comments on rugby league, but he had to agree she had a point all the same.

"I do not expect you to take to the idea straight away, madame" said Seth. "I visualise a lot of opposition to the scheme, naturally. You are bound to have fears and reservations. I could expect nothing else. But think of the long term. Believe me, Jaques and I are investing in the future. Yes, we are in it for business reasons – I am a business man first and foremost but Jaques is also a fanatical rugby league man and I know he would never withdraw his support."

"That's as mebbe", muttered Phoebe Maud, munching yet another chocolate biscuit with great relish.

Joshua's stomach started making rumbling noises and his water works were shouting out for him to make a lavatorial excursion. He was a nervous animal despite his bravado and 'hail fellow well met' manner. Just what was that little tarted up chap who spoke with a plum in his gob wanting him to do? Joshua could never understand how prime ministers and potentates managed, they must have nerves of steel – here he was breaking wind and bursting for a slash, the old symptoms. The doctor put it down to the joint worry of running a rugby club and a textile mill. He excused himself and headed out of the back door and down the cobbled yard to the wooden W.C. Stuck behind the pipes was a daily paper torn up into handy sizes.

"Featherstone Rovers in deep trouble" ran the headlines on one

11

page. The article stated that Rovers were having a lot of problems getting a team together for the re-commencement of the season of peace-time Rugby League. Like Bramfield, their ground needed a lot of repairs. The article went on to mention Bruddersby Stanley who had asked their players to accept a pound less for winning money away from home. Three of the players had asked for transfers. If only the league had a magic wand, conjectured Joshua, as he gazed up at the galaxy through the hole in the roof. Just what was on offer from this foreign geezer? But Northern folks didn't take to foreigners. It wasn't natural somehow.

When he returned to the table he found his wife was enjoying the gushing charm of the tripe king and still tucking in to the chocolate biscuits. "He could sell ice to the bloody Eskimos, this mon' thought Joshua to himself. He'd have to be a ruddy good salesman to sell his idea of a Super League to the hard headed chairmen of the clubs. They'd tell him where to stick his ideas, that was for certain. They call a spade a spade in Leigh and Castleford, no messing.

"Can I ask you to think over the idea, Mr. Hepplethwaite? That is all I ask. But just remember this – the future of the rugby league depends on money. Basic fact of life and from what I'm told on the business grapevine, a lot of clubs are being financed by rich men who know nothing of the game but like to be at the helm of a club. Power. Monsieur Chevalier can see the day when these gentlemen will give way to men of vision, to men paid salaries to coach players. Professional managers who will be responsible for the running of the club and the team. In a word, sir, the code needs a flow of cash.

"Now sir, gaze out of the window. It's a Saturday afternoon – not winter time yet, but it's pouring down – typical English weather. Just think what it will be doing round these parts in deep winter. Balaclava helmets, hot water bottles stuck down trousers, thermos flasks full of hot cocoa, typical rugby league weather with the fans frozen to the bone".

12

"And how can we stop that ?" asked Joshua. "Can your French bloke change the weather ? He'll make a hell of a lot more money doing that than ever he will out of his onions !"

"He can't change the weather, but he can alter the conditions by switching the game to the spring and summer months ."

"Summer rugby! " exploded Joshua, "You must be rudddy balmy!"

"Why not ? Think of it. Instead of shivering in freezing weather the spectators can bask in the warm sunshine away from the bitter winds that blow across the Pennines, winds that would take the skin off your back, hail stones as big as golf balls pelting down; frozen legs, chilblains, chesty coughs, they'd all be things of the past."

"You may claim to be a northerner, Seth ould lad, but you don't think like one. If there's one thing a Northerner likes more than anything else its a bloody good moan! They put up with all that stuff just so they can belly ache about it. Do you want to take all us pleasures away? And there's summat else you're forgetting. What about our great love of cricket? Why, Lancashire and Yorkshire league grounds are packed on a good day watching Leary Constantine and all them Indian lads that come over as pro's. You can't watch rugby and cricket int' same afternoon tha' knows".

"Our idea eliminates the problem. Our U.C.P. Super League will play on Sundays".

If Halifax Town Hall clock had suddenly fallen at his size twelve feet Joshua could not have been more astonished, he blew hard into his red spotted handkerchief – it was all he could do. Words failed him. For once verbosity was nullified. After a pause of at least two minutes all he could say was "Well, I'll go to our 'ouse on a bicycle made for two! If that don't take the biscuit I don't know what does. I'd keep these ideas to yourself, owd lad, if you don't want lynching and hanging from the goal posts at Watershedding".

"That is the chance Monsieur Chevalier and myself are willing to take and we hope you will join us on a joint podium to address the club chairmen, Mister Hepplethwaite."

"You've as much chance as persuading a Widnes fan to give money to a Wires player's benefit fund." And with that parting shot the Bramfield chairman rose to his full six feet and waddled his sixteen stones plus frame out of the tripe rooms in disbelief at all he had heard. Mrs. Hepplethwaite made her apologies and hastily followed her husband still nibbling a chocolate biscuit.

"The blokes off his rocker love. I reckon as his minds been affected by the war. We'll hear no more about it you mark my words."

"Oh I don't think so Josh love. He's deadly serious. You're minds blinkered to progress. you can't see woods for trees".

"Progress! Call that progress? You're as bad as him Phoebe Maud".

Seth asked Mabel to pour him a brandy out of the hospitality bottle they kept behind the aspidistra for medicinal reasons and smiled to himself at Joshua's reactions. Typical. Dyed in the wool traditionalist but if a northerner smells brass then he can be lured into the net.

Somehow he felt the woman was on his side. Joshua was a different kettle of fish but he could be persuaded.

"I wonder if he has an Achilles heel?" he asked himself aloud.

"I don't know owt about that, but he had an umbrella", replied Mabel, brusquely Ewbanking the linoleum.

Mr. Scragbottom felt a warm glow. He had sown the seeds and he was quietly confident they would germinate. Those chocolate biscuits would prove to be worth their weight in gold. Always get on the good side of the woman of the house was a good old motto in business and he was sure it would hold good now. Time would tell. If Hepplethwaite failed then he would seek out Barnacre. He would go to every chairman in the league if he had to.

Chapter 2

It was business once again back at the mill for Joshua the next day. Miss Hyacinth Grimshaw was preparing his favourite 'cockle warmer', rum and coffee, when the phone rang.

It was one of those contraptions that required winding up by a handle for at least half a minute before the speaker's voice could be heard. Even then it sounded as though the speaker was in China and not down the road.

"Mr. Hepplethwaite's secretary speaking. Can I be of assistance? Do you wish discourse on matters appertaining to the mill or do you refer to matters relating to Bramfield Rugby League Football Club?"

Joshua chuckled to himself. He loved having a secretary who could match anyone for posh talk. She was worth every bit of the four quid a week he paid her, even though it was ten bob over the top. Like a lot of well educated women she had joined the land army to "lend a hand on the land". Now she was back at the mill again.

"A Mr. Scragbottom for you, Mr. Hepplethwaite. Sounds very important. Speaks like a real gentleman."

"Oh aye ? He's a persistent beggar is that lad".

The Onion King proceeded to remind Joshua about the benefits his club, and all the clubs, would receive under the proposed new league structure. He pointed out that there would be all kinds of perks, and that he, Joshua, would go down in history as the man who brought the game of rugby league into the twentieth century. According to the sponsors the game was still in the dark ages etc. etc.... 'Owd' Josh couldn't get a word in edgeways and in the end promised to bring the matter up with his co-directors when he met them up at the ground that evening.

He had enough worries as it was. He was dying for a pee again, always a sign that the old anxiety was at him. Why the bloody hell did he have to meet up with Seth Scragbottom and his crazy ideas? It was bad enough coping with the fact that the orders for army blankets and shirts had finished. It was peace time again and it would be back to normal trading at t'mill – that's if business got back to what it was before the war. He'd have to go on the knocker again. It was a new age opening up after the long dismal austerity but times wouldn't just get better at the wave of a wand. Until he knew how business was going to be he wouldn't be able to sink any brass into the club. It was like when you got wed, a twopenny pie costs fourpence. 'Appen Rovers would have to do like they do in Wigan, do without. But hang on! 'Appen there is a magic wand. 'Appen this crazy idea of a Super League could catch on? If these two fellows have so much brass why not relieve 'em of it? If only someone else could put it to the rest of the chairmen. There were some hard nosed characters amongst them and he'd feel a right 'narna' going to Hadfield Barnacre, for instance. Old Barney Thistlethwaite of Barrow would tell him to go to hell that was for sure.

He threw a bucket of coke on the fire and sat up close. June? That was a laugh. It was bitter cold. Still, he had to admit it could take up any time. Summer rugby? They'd think he'd come up the Irwell on a banana boat if he suggested that!

Scragbottom was right, though, about the awful weather conditions. He felt sorry for the wingers stuck out on the flanks unable to get into the game for long periods. He reckoned they might approve of it but it would be like asking a dog not to chase cats to persuade most folk. They don't like change, that's it. The devil you know and all that stuff. . .'Appen he'd ask owd Tubby Branbottom from Bramley to broach it . . . but no . . he'd have to face music himself or tell Scragbottom to make other arrangements. Just then Miss Grimshaw called him over to her office.

"I've just had a call from the police station, Mr. Hepplethwaite. Chief Superintendent Grim. He's very concerned about the crater on the north terrace at Marl Heights. The one the German plane made when its wing was shot off during that dog fight. He says he couldn't allow rugby to be played at the ground until it was filled in. He said they hadn't bothered in the war time Emergency League due to the small numbers of spectators but he feared it could be a very dangerous hazard in peace time rugby. I assured him you would give the matter your urgent consideration."

Bloody hell! More brass. Well, he'd have to discuss it with his co directors. 'Appen they'd think of summat.

That evening Joshua was at Marl Heights, the ground played on by his beloved Rovers. Co-directors Bob and Bert Kearsley were having a cup of tea with him as they all gazed out of a dirty stained window in the club house.

"Look at the state of this window, it's turning black" said Bert Kearsley, a portly man who always sported a flamboyant dicky bow.

"It's weather up here", said brother Bob, a man with a penchant for pickles and known in the game as "Pickles Kearsley".

"It's Anno Domino more than likely. We've had it since club house were built, thirty three year ago come last whit week". The two brothers nodded in agreement at Joshua's remark. Old age was knackering every thing at the ground and the arctic blasts from Blackstone Edge didn't help. Marl Heights rivalled Siberia on winter Saturday afternoons.

Joshua's thoughts wandered to the great players who had graced the field of play. Ghosts flitted across the grass before him. . . the bulky Jim Sullivan, kicking a goal from the half way line; mercurial Alf Ellaby, the St. Helen's flash, dancing down the touch line; little Tommy McCue the Widnes scrum half genius weaving his way to the try line; the 'terrible trio' of Smith, Fildes and Mulvanney of St. Helen's Recs. He wouldn't see the Recs again. They had shut down for good when the war started. What memories he had – how the crowd had howled when Cumberbatch the Barrow flyer had scored the winning try from a forward pass – bloody hell, the ref was lucky to escape that day! Chris Brereton, the Leeds prop was

17

lucky not to get lynched after he'd had a set to with Barney Jones . . . but that was rugby league; blame the ref for everything and don't give any credit to the opposition. All speccies are the same. He'd seen some great players during the war as well when the Emergency League had been in existence. Dewsbury under Eddie Waring had the pick of the players available and some fine displays they'd put up at Marl Heights. The make shift Rovers had been mangled into the ground but he'd never forget the great performance put up by the gallant youngsters who held Dewsbury to a four all draw with a minute to run. Then Roy Francis, 'the dusty aristocrat', had struck with the speed and elusiveness of an electric eel running through the entire Rovers team to score under the posts. He'd be glad to welcome 'gentleman Roy' back to Marl Heights, in the colours of his old club Barrow, back again after war time closure.

"Are you cogitating, Josh, owd spud?" asked Bert. "We've seen some great games on this field and 'appen we will again although what sort of team we'll be able to field I've no idea. Stanley Keithley is down in Wales scouting and he says he's got two likely lads who are prepared to come up for little pay as long as we can give 'em work. Trouble is we haven't got t'brass to buy International Union men."

"We'll have to encourage local talent, brother Bert" said Bob, helping himself to one of his pickles.

"We're holding trials on Saturday" said Joshua. "We'll see what turns up. We've had some belting finds from t'local leagues in the past."

"Lets hope we do again" said Bert, pronging a pickle with the club pickle fork. Even that was badly bent and on its last legs.

"All t'brass we get through turnstiles will have to be spent on doing ground up." Bert's statement rang very true. In the old days Stanley Keighley, the local undertaker, who acted as scout, would go down to Wales and often as not come up with an R.U. concert, and some belters they'd had and all. No, it looked as if local talent and 'has beens' would have to be the mainspring of the club for a while. Bob was doing a calculation in a little book. He'd acted as secretary since they had been forced to get rid of the paid man. Bob was also acting treasurer as well.

"What's up, our Bob?" asked Bert who could always tell when his brother had a knotty problem.

"It's the bloody ground; and that's swearing by a chap who doesn't swear. It were alreet letting the field out to that farmer bloke but his goats have devastated the place. They couldn't get out onto the terraces, or so we thought, so they ate their way out and they've chewed all wood at the front of best stand; and look at them weeds over yon on south banking. Why, they've got roots as long as our overdraft at bank. They'll all need pulling up and the whole bank needs shoring up and reinforcing with steel girders. No wonder that bobby rang you Josh – I reckon as he'll make a proper inspection and find lots of jobs needing doing. The fence needs fettlin' and all . . . it's a bleak outlook, gentlemen . . . bleak indeed."

Joshua gave a cough, which was half of embarrassment and half because one of Bob's pickles had gone down the wrong way. He had something to say and he felt nervous about it.

"What's wrong Josh, old Prater? Summat up?" asked Bert.

Joshua rose to his feet in trepidation. "I need to pick my words very carefully gentlemen. Let me say that a certain person who shall be nameless for the moment, has approached me with a scheme to pump money into rugby league. His partner, a Frenchman, has come up with a revolutionary idea. It's hard to swallow, although I don't know all the ins and outs yet, but basically it means the formation of what they call a Super League in which our clubs will compete not only against each other but against the french clubs".

"Yer what!" stormed Bob who was a traditionalist after the old school.

"Play against bloody frogs! Never! You can't trust foreigners. Look what the Germans got up to. Why, Lancashire and Yorkshire folk can't get on. Never mind English and French. You'll be asking us to speak to cockneys next."

"What sort of money are they on about, Joshua"? asked Bert seriously. Like a true northerner the smell of 'brass' excited him.

"I don't know t'full story. But I've been told as this consortium what's forming are out to promote business – a joint venture of English tripe and trotters and French onions. They want to call the league the U.C.P. Super League. They say they'll do up all the grounds and club houses – give every club a grant. No strings attached. There'll be travelling money provided for clubs playing in France. There's a dozen and one other things too – rules and benefits, but it's all in't air yet. The Englishman in the consortium, Seth Scragbottom, the tripe king, (I've let his name out of t'bag, now) wants me to sound out the club chairmen and if they are interested, call a meeting of them and hear the proposals."

"I've never heard owt so balmy" rasped Bob. "Don't tell me you're in favour, our Bert? I'm surprised at thee!"

"Money talks, Bob. Just imagine what we could do if ground were done up. I mean, we've had complaints from visiting clubs about the changing rooms, the locals reckon the drains are blocked up and causing a hell of a stink in t'local council estate. It'll all get worse, nowt surer our Bob. Nowts surer, it'll get worse.

Then, when all is put reet we could send Keighley down to Wales to buy some established union men – I reckon as there'll be a rush up north now the war's over. Only trouble is wealthy clubs like Huddersfield, Leeds and Wigan will get t'cream."

"Well, what do you think Bob? Are you prepared that I should go ahead as your chairman and representative and seek out the other clubs? No harm in seeing what's on offer is there. We don't have to buy it."

"Well, I suppose so, Joshua, but I don't like this French connection. Can't we just deal with the Englishman?"

"Nay Bob. It's both of 'em or nowt. They're in it together."

"All reet Joshua lad, but be damned careful what thee does! Let's open that bottle of Scotch and have some pickles. It's fair got me worked up".

Joshua stayed on into the twilight hours still gazing out across the old pitch, shadows adding to the mystique and nostalgia associated with a ground that had become famous in the Rugby League. Many a whippet had cocked its leg on the old fence, aye, and many a speccie had peed where he stood, too lazy to go to the stinking tin roofed lavatory to relieve himself . . . They were rum lads, league fans, die-hards, grumbled like bloody hell, but they always stuck by the team in their darkest hours. Surely all the character would go out of the game if big business got hold of it; there was an earthiness about the game that had its roots way back in tried and trusted Northern values. They'd be selling folks down the river . . . . could he trust big business to keep those values? He doubted it. After another glass of the Black Market Scotch he wended his way home.

"It'll be nice to get back to the old ways, Joshua lad" remarked a neighbour as he walked up the garden path.

"Aye, 'appen so Fred . . . . but we never know what's round next corner, owd lad."

"What's biting Joshua, he looks worried does the lad" said Fred to his missus when he got in the house.

It was the next morning. Joshua was tucking into a plate full of fried bread and black puddings. Phoebe Maud was dusting the aspidistra and singing a chorus of *'When the Sun has got his Hat on'* the latest Jack Hylton hit record.

"Bob Kearsley thinks I'm a reet pudding" said Joshua at last.

He can't see further than his nose that lad" said Phoebe Maud. "But what can you expect from a chap that won't go further south than Warrington if he can help it? He's hardly likely to take to the idea of playing French teams and extending the game down south, is he?"

"Are you for it then, lass?"

"Nay, but, well, I rather took to Mr. Scragbottom. He's sort o' genteel and sensitive, not like some folk round here. He knows

21

how to look after a lass . . . considerate and gentlemanly."

"You mean I'm not?"

"I wasn't meaning you, love".

"Oh aye, who was it then ? Next door's moggy ?"

"Don't take on, Josh love. You're not exactly a Rudolph Valentino are you but I love you just as you are. What do you reckon to him, then?"

"He's a Lancashire lad that's got ideas above his station. He's gone posh. He's a very wealthy fellar and I suppose as he's travelled a lot. As my old mother used to say he's 'peas above sticks', the way he talks doesn't go with being in tripe business does it?"

"That's why he wants you to negotiate for him love. He's looking to the future, Joshua. There's no harm in doing up all the shops like he suggests and taking tripe and trotters to the masses. It's the better off market he's after, tripe's always been a working man's dish. That George Orwell painted an awful picture when he described that tripe shop he lodged at in Wigan – flies all over the place and bugs crawling over the tripe. It were in that book *The Road to Wigan Pier*".

"Aye, you're right there love" agreed Josh . "That Orwell's about as popular in Wigan as Jack Arkwright was when he were playing for t'Wire".

Just then the phone rang.

"Hepplethwaite residence" announced Phoebe Maud. "Oh it's you, Mr. Scragbottom. I'll just get my Joshua".

"Hepplethwaite here . . . . no, I haven't made me mind up yet. It's a very big decision to make. I've told my co-directors and there was a mixed reception. One of 'em thought I'd lost me marbles. We can see that money is badly needed to do up the grounds but if I do get the club chairmen together – and I'm not promising I will, think on – there's going to be all hell let loose and thousands of questions asked. And what are these radical changes your French bloke has in mind? Oh I know you just want to get them all together to explain the project . . .yer what? . . ee . . . well . . . we like us chuck . . . .

22

I'll have to think about it . . . hang on, I'll ask the missus . . . . that's her department".

Joshua put his large mitt over the tube and whispered to his wife. "He's offering us free tripe and other pig products if I'll approach the chairmen. What will I do luv?"

"Ask him how long for".

"The wife says how long for? For life? Well . . . I don't know . . . . 'appen that'll be long enough . . . I'll just ask her what she wants". . .

"Two cow heels, a plate o' thick seam and three trotters every Friday tell him" rattled his missus.

Joshua repeated Phoebe's order to the great tripe king.

"He says that's fine, lass. He'll instruct local branch to deliver it weekly . . What shall I do lass? Ee, I'm not sure really . . . what will rest of the league think? Hang on Mr. Scragbottom . . . . I can't do it, lass, what shall I tell him? I'm in a proper quandary".

"Tell him to throw in a pigs foot and it's a deal", came the reply.

Seth replaced the phone and poured himself a brandy to celebrate the surmounting of the first hurdle. Joshua spoke the same language as the league hierarchy. He would be the ideal mediator.

"I knew Hepplethwaite had an Achilles heel . . .and a cow heel at that, ha ha! It is now up to my French partner and myself to educate our rugby league moguls to go into Europe and progress. After that who knows?"

He wound up the handle of the telephone and dialled for trunks. "Put me through to Mr. Chevalier, please, young lady. Paris, France, 66967584. Person to person call."

After a thirty minutes wait and much handle winding a crackling voice was heard speaking in broken English, "Jaques speaking . . . . pardonez moi? Monsieur Apple Tree will do it! Bon! You have done well my friend!

Excellentay! The world is our oyster! . . . . Am I correct? I will have to improve my English . . . Qui?"

23

Joshua addresses the league chairmen

Chapter 3

Joshua had chosen Cleckheaton for the venue of the meeting of the R.F.L. and club chairmen and directors. Just one week to the very day he had met Seth Scragbottom here he was sitting on a makeshift podium composed of beer crates in the local branch of the Cloggers and Bottom Knockers Social Club (affiliated). A picked assembly were present composed of directors, chairmen and secretaries as well as members of the press eager for news. Two other men shared the podium with Josh: Seth the English sponsor and Jonah Hawksbody the narrow minded secretary of the R.F.L. Jonah's surname suited him ideally, for he had the appearance of a cadaverous bird of prey sitting on a branch waiting for a victim. There was more humour in a dry stick.

Joshua's stomach was turning over like a mill wheel. Before him was a sea of faces, a mixture of business men and hard-as-nails directors whose main concern was brass in the pocket. If they had been Bedouin tribesmen Joshua could not have been more nervous.

"Look at their bloody faces" he whispered to Seth nervously.

"Like Watersheddings on a wet day". Certainly they were a dour bunch and it was no wonder the Bramfield chairman quaked at the task ahead of him. Why did Phoebe Maud have to be so fond of tripe and trotters? If Seth hadn't dangled such irresistible bait he wouldn't be in this mess. She'd do owt for tripe would the lass.

After a throat-clearing cough, Joshua rose to his feet:

"Mr. Hawksbody, fellow chairmen and directors of the Rugby League; it is my task to introduce you to a visiting gentleman who will address the assembly. I know a lot of you, and most of you know me – and you may be thinking what's this man up to? What I've done in acting as a mediator is in the interests of rugby league as a game and in its future. The war in Europe is over. As you can see the bunting is still up in the club after the V.D. Day celebrations a few weeks ago..."

A bony elbow was thrust in his ribs as the secretary of the league whispered in his ear.

"Ee, I'm sorry... it's were a fox's pass, as the French say. I should have said V.E. Day. Where was I? Oh, aye . . . the war is over. Germany is defeated and I know we all hope and pray our lads will soon polish off the opposition in the Far East as well..." A few 'ear ears' and isolated claps greeted the remark. "And lets hope our country will once more be great in peace as it was in war. Lets hope rugby league will grow in popularity and esteem and that young lads will continue to fill our clubs with talent and . . ."

"Get on with it, Joshua lad" bellowed old Bob Halfpenny of Widnes.

"Hang on Bob old sport" retorted Joshua. "I were only wishing us all well... but... well... sometimes... times change and many folk don't like change . . ." Joshua was stumbling now.

"You've sold us down t'river to a ruddy frog!" shouted out Arnold Fish of Liverpool Stanley, a man with six chins and brewer's droop. "There's been rumours all week about it. Come, Mr. Hepplethwaite, lets have it straight from t'horses mouth. What's going on ?"

This remark brought forth cheers and foot stamping. Joshua put his huge hand up for silence. It was a full minute before he got it.

"Aw reet! It isn't easy standing here and as I said I'm doing it in the best interests of the game . . ."

"And your pocket I'll venture". This interruption came from Hadfield Barnacre of Bruddersby, Joshua's hated rival who never missed a chance to get a dig in at the Bramfield chairman.

"That were below the belt lad! Are you still shooting pigeons?"* This last remark of Joshua's referred to an incident several years before when Hadfield had shot down Bramfield's pigeons on the way to the newspaper offices after a home game. At this point Jonah Hawksbody intervened, his face like thunder.

"I'll warn you two once only – I'll have none of your antics! Couple of trouble makers you are."

Joshua shot an evil look at Hadfield and continued. "Well, all it remains for me to do now is to introduce you to Mr. Scragbottom of the U.C.P. but before I do so I note that the bar is open and so why don't you lads all get a pint a-piece before he addresses you. After his address there will be an interval for more ale and some food and I'm pleased to tell you that I've engaged Samuel Butt, by kind permission of the Shunters Club, who will give a ferret juggling exhibition. Sam has recently come back from a tour for E.N.S.A. entertaining troops and war workers in factories. And now, after you've all got your ale in, Mr. Scragbottom will give you the full details of his proposed Super League. So get supping, lads."

"Who's ale is it ? Not French muck I hope" was one remark.

"You're lucky to get ale at all" retorted Joshua. "Didn't you know we've just had a war? It was in all the papers."

Somewhat pacified by Ogden's best bitter which Joshua had almost gone down on his bended knees for, beer being strictly rationed, the assembly settled down to listen to what the tripe king had to say. A deep silence reigned as he unfolded his plan. Many were too dumbfounded to reply anyway. He spoke for a full hour and was only finally halted when someone shouted "Pies have come!"

"He's said a lot and said nowt" was the opinion of Bert Bradbottle of Leeds as he munched a Holland's pie. "No one does

see put ref a jersey on!   27

owt for nowt" said Bob Houghton of Oldham. "Free ale and pies – why I haven't seen a Holland's pie for four years, they're up to summat. French money buying us cheap to sell us down the river."

"Well don't eat it then" said Joshua who had joined Bob at the bar. To a man who had been on one pie a week during rationing it was like asking a dog not to wag its tail. "Well, what do you think, seriously Bob?". Bob took off his hard hat to polish it with spit.

"I want to know a hell of a lot more Josh. We need brass in the clubs, all of us. Rank disrepair in most grounds now after the lay off. Furthermore we need it for players. They say as a lot of Welsh lads will come north – we're all after a Gus Risman or two aren't we? But we can't buy 'em for nowt. So I'd welcome an injection of capital; but it's second half of his speech I'm interested in – the new structure he talks about and the do's and don'ts."

"I think you've summed up the feeling of all of us" seconded Fred Mumps of Bramley downing his pint in one gulp. "Lets eat us pies anyhow and sup the ale . . . that's summat at least. We can always say no and sod off home". Fred's down to earth remark brought grunts of approval. Then it was time for the entertainer, more ale, and a chorus of Land of Hope and Glory before Seth once more climbed on to the podium. When all was quiet he announced:

"The new Super League will be made up as follows, bearing in mind my previous remarks and observations about amalgamations and mergers of certain clubs. Some clubs are able to go it alone, others, for their own good, will have to merge in order to survive. Make notes if you wish, gentlemen. I ask the gentlemen of the press gathered here on this auspicious occasion to inform their readers that U.C.P. (being a merger of English and French business interests for the good of culinary art and the betterment of all digestive systems) have not made the decisions lightly. Great thought has gone into the selections of the clubs for the new Super League. Listen closely gentlemen. I am quite happy to repeat any statement afterwards for the papers. And now scribes of the British press, and those who have come over from the French newspapers,

28

Leeds R.L.F.C. directors travelling to meeting at Cleckheaton please have your inkwells filled and your nibs at the ready. Chairmen of the Rugby League this is your Super League: "

The proverbial pin did not drop but if it had done so it would have sounded like the stentorian roar of a lion – such was the deep pregnant expectancy of the drama-charged atmosphere. The Cloggers and Bottom Knockers Club had never known anything like it before. The first suggested merger staggered the assembly!

"Wigan – St. Helens. No doubt to be known as the Saintly Pie Eaters" (Seth allowed himself a wry smile).

Leeds – Batley also to merger. There was a pause as pandemonium broke out in the auditorium . . . .

Bramley, to remain the same.

Keighley to stay as they are.

Dieppe Garlic and Shallot Company – being the club belonging to Monsieur Chevalier.

Paris Moulin Rouge Rovers, a newly formed club.

Toulouse Tacklers.

London Chemicals – being an amalgamation of the old Streatham and Mitcham club and Widnes. The sponsors are currently negotiating with the english rugby union for the use of Twickenham for home games. Severe strictures regarding the wearing of correct dress will be enforced at this ground. Items such as bags of sticky boiled sweets and sherbet will be removed at the turnstiles, as will flat caps, clogs and chewing tobacco.

Yull. This club will replace the old Hull teams and York and will play at Robin Hoods Bay to attract holiday makers.

Dewslet – a merger of Dewsbury and Hunslet.

Leigh – Broughton. Merger of two Manchester area clubs.

Holyhead Hornets. Rochdale to merge with the welsh rugby union club who are going professional under the Super League. Matches to be played at Holyhead but kick off times will be subject to tides. Excursions to and from Dublin will be arranged for all home matches.

Stanley Wires. Liverpool Stanley to join forces with Warrington to play at New Brighton, that thriving holiday town on the River Mersey. The beauty of summer rugby being that crowds of holiday makers, so far alien to rugby league, will learn to love our sport. In this way it will spread.

Swinford. Swinton and Salford. Venue for matches yet to be finalised. Douglas, Isle of Man, is a possible venue if we can get a kipper franchise.

Huddersfield. This old club being domiciled in the town which played host to the formation of the Rugby League will keep its own identity.

Barrowfield. Barrow and Wakefield. This new club will play at St. Albans where a new purpose-built stadium will be erected. The sponsors feel that this hitherto untapped area will be a growth area for the code.

Featherfax. As the name implies Featherstone Rovers and Halifax. They will move to Inverness and play under the sponsorship of the Harry Lauder Haggis and Bagpipe Company, a subsidiary of U.C.P. All spectators must wear kilts.

Castleford. We feel after long deliberations that it is better to let this club stand alone as the sponsors feel that rioting could break out in this hot bed of traditionalism and deep yorkshire pride.

Bruddersby and Bramfield to join forces as Bramersley Athletic. Both grounds will be kept so that alternate home matches can be featured. We feel this is only fair in order to appease both Yorkshire and Lancashire spectators.

Isle of Sark. Channel Island club who feel they have a lot to offer the Super League. Bird watching weekends will be arranged as part of a package for visiting supporters.

French Foreign Legion. This regiment possessing some of the toughest men in the world in its ranks is joining the Super League. The Super League have obtained amnesties for all criminals on the run from justice who have taken refuge in the Legion.

Bradford Northern will change its name to Bradford Trotters. The

U.C.P. in conjunction with Monsieur Chevalier have negotiated with Bradford council for the sale of the site of the ground – a huge area. This along with the rugby club will house the worlds biggest tripe emporium. Hence the club being called the Trotters instead of Northern.

Finally, another French club. A town well known for obvious reasons to millions of Britishers – Dunkirk Trinity.

The fixture list is in the process of being drawn up but I can give you the matches for the first day of the New Super league. "I will now give you a break in order to fill your inkwells gentlemen and change nibs if necessary, and of course to discuss what I have said."

"We have also negotiated with the representatives of clubs and proposed clubs wishing to take up rugby league. These include The Vatican, The Salvation Army and Accrington Stanley. Negotiations are also underway with the M.C.C. who are considering the possibility of turning the gentlemens enclosure into a tripe restaurant."

For a minute or two it was like waiting for a bomb to explode. Not a word was uttered – stunned amazement reigned in the hearts and minds of all in the room. They could only gaze at one another with blank faces.

It is not in the power of this scribe, dear reader, to put into words the reaction to the structure of the proposed League. I prefer to leave it to writers of greater literary talent than my own to chronicle it for posterity. In a word they were gobsmacked.

For once, however, Joshua Parkinson Hepplethwaite and Hadfield Plantagenet Barnacre were in total agreement.

"We're not bloody having it!" they roared in unison at Mr. Scragbottom, their faces puce in colour.

"But my co-sponsor in France has gone into great detail why your two clubs should join forces – both communities will benefit."

"What, Yorkshire and Lancashire blending together! Yon mon,

Monsewer Chefsalleyway, knows nowt about it! It's like asking Hitler to share a bed with Churchill. Oil and wayter don't mix and I'm surprised at thee being a Rochdale man agreeing to such a proposal. Sod that for a game of sowjers!"

"Your point has been noted" boomed Jonah Hawksbody in his sermonizing tones. "Kindly sit down Mr. Hepplethwaite!"

Joshua was so angry that when he did sit his eighteen stones frame almost wrecked the podium and Jonah fell off at one end and dropped his Hollands Pie into the club cat's water bucket. For once in his life Hadfield had to agree that Joshua was right. The very idea!

The meeting had begun at noon and it was now six o'clock. The fury of the chairmen required to amalgamate was red hot and feverish. Mr. Scragbottom was a cool customer, give him his due, love him or hate him. Not one inch would he budge. It was a question of don't do as you are told and you won't get the very considerable money. The amount of one thousand pounds to each club was something the chairmen could hardly refuse and they were assured that further sums would be put into the club's coffers as the Super League progressed. Barrowfield, who were to move to St. Albans, would have a brand new ground provided for them, purpose built by an army of builders from France. Joshua was sweating profusely and his bladder was playing him up something rotten. He turned to the tripe king in anger.

"Thy's buggered up my sphincter with all this to do. It's fair fettling my nerves all this. I wouldn't have done it if I'd known there was going to be all this hulla balloo and belly aching".

"We empire builders have to have nerves of steel, Mr. Hepplethwaite", was the reply from the tripe king who didn't appear to have a nerve in his whole body. "Nil Carborundum, or don't let the blighters grind you down as the saying goes".

"That might be alright for thee, Mr. Scragbottom, but I'm a man of the people first and a business man second. You and Mr. Chefsalleyway think money can buy anything and anybody. You can't mess with tradition. Try to ride roughshod over the speccies and you'll come off second best. You don't care about the collier what's been down the pit all week slaving away, his only relief from the drudgery thinking about his beloved Halifax or Leigh. He doesn't go to the match to watch a game of rugby, he goes to watch his team and win, lose or draw he won't shift his allegiance, and this summer rugby is a load of old cobblers! And what you and that French mate don't understand is that Northerners love a bit of suffering. Oh aye, they'll moan like hell about the cold wind and the hail stones but deep inside of 'em they like standing there on the banking sucking an old Betty Plant's Winter Warmer with a hot water bottle stuffed down their kecks!"

A round of applause greeted Joshua's outburst. But Hadfield Barnacre wasn't impressed with Joshua's show of loyalty.

"He's hunting with the hounds and running with the hare. A foot in two camps, that's Hepplethwaite. He's after brass like all Lancastrians."

It was now Jonah Hawksbody's turn to get his two-penn'orth in and what he said came as no surprise.

"I've listened with interest to the arguments for and against and I'm quite happy to discuss it further when we all meet in Leeds with the Rugby League Council. But there's one thing I will never agree to and that's playing on the Lord's day. I can assure you, Mr. Scragbottom, that the Lord's Day Observance Society will not allow such sacrilege. We will fight you tooth and nail!"

"Then all I can say to you, Mr. Hawksbody, is that if you are a man of principal then you should resign. But enough of this for the moment. U.C.P. have laid on a knife and fork tea for you all and I ask you to remain seated, gentlemen, so the waitresses can serve the tripe and onions – compliments of course of the sponsors of the Super League". Mr Scragbottom had said his piece.

The grumbling rose to heights of agitation Joshua had never before encountered even though he had taken part in many important meetings of the league chairmen. "I've opened a reet can of ruddy worms" he confided to Herbert Grimley, a brewer from Hull.

"Hey up Josh, here comes trouble lad" whispered Herbert. The bumptious figure of Bluddersbys chairman was heading towards them. Small and round, he waddled like a pregnant duck and his cold fish-like eyes boded no good to his rival from Bramfield.

"I'm told he were a right swine in the Home Guard, captain he was" said the Hull man with a smirk.

"He'd be nowt' less would Barnacre" said Joshua. "Pompous little dictator he is. Did you hear him accuse me?" Hadfield glared at them.

"Now look here Hepplethwaite!" Hadfield didn't stand on ceremony, he went for Joshua like a little fearless terrier attacking a bull.

"Who the hell are you talking to?" retorted Josh.

"To you, who else?"

"Oh I see. Well, I'm not one of your bloody snotty nosed privates in your Home Guard unit. The wars over, furthermore I'm a mill owner like you and a chairman of a club. The names MISTER Hepplethwaite so kindly use it".

"Some representative of Rugby League you are, egging on these two business men. Can't you see they're only in it for what they can get out of it. They're steamrolling us," ranted Hadfield.

"I told you I were the mediator at beginning. Have you got cloth ears? We don't have to accept it and believe me you're the last chap I'd like to sit on a board with. I'm with you against the amalgamation any road. What you grinning at?"

The cynical smile always infuriated Joshua, he could accept honest to goodness ignorance from anyone but this odious little man irritated him almost beyond belief.

"I'm laughing at your deceit Joshua owd lad. You stand there and pretend there's nowt in it for you. Why I think as you and this U.C.P. man have planned this. Lancastrians never do owt for nowt anyway that's common knowledge."

"Ee ... that's choice coming from a Tyke! If we're tight then we

35

learned it all from your lot. As for me getting summat out of it financially then its all in your imagination. And don't you knock Lancastrians. Where would England be without the red rose? Best cricketers, best brass bands . . ."

"Best braggers!" retorted Hadfield going red in the face. By this time a small knot of chairmen and officials had gathered round. The confrontation between the two men was as furious as the confrontations between the two teams they represented.

"I'm not bragging. I've no need. Look at any club and you'll see that Lancashire excels. We're cleverest at rugby and all . . . more Yorkshire men get sent off than Lancashire . . ."

"Rubbish! I'll make you swallow that remark . . . and I hope it chokes you! You say as we're tight, well wait while I tell yer . . . the tightest folks in the north come from Oldham. They'd split matches in two . . . you ask 'em in Blackpool. It's not the Scots what's noted for meanness, its the rough necks from Oldham."

"Bloody lies! They're salt of the earth. Best natured and kindest folk on Gods earth. The meanest man in England was from Heckmondwyke – It's in Ripleys 'Book of Facts and Freaks' is that. He were called Oswald Skinaflea, that's how the word skinflint came about. When he were a young 'un he dreamed of being a miser. 'Cause he'd met so many, being born in the 'don't do owt for now't' county. But he wanted to be the best of 'em all so he decides to go to an island a mile off Whitby where a famous miser lived..."

"There's no island near to Whitby, you're a liar". bellowed Hadfield. But Joshua wasn't being put off.

"Appen Yorkshire sold it cause it were there according to this book. So Oswald goes over on a rowing boat to meet this great miser hoping to learn a lot. The old chap is sitting warming himself by a candle counting his money. Young Oswald takes his pants off." "What are you doing that for?" asked the miser surprised like.

"I'm not sitting down in me pants, I'll wear 'em out" says Oswald, being a true Yorkshire mon.

"Young man" says the miser, "You can go home on the next boat. I can't teach you anything!"

"A likely ruddy tale. . .he's full of bull shit is Hepplethwaite. ." The shadow of the gaunt Jonah Hawksbody fell across the group "I'll not tolerate such language Mr Barnacre – gentlemen kindly take your seats for the meal. And as for both of you I'm sick to death of your haggling and outbursts. If we do join in the Super League this sort of behaviour will not be tolerated. Think on!"

Everyone had to agree that it was a right good 'do'. The one thing everyone craved for at the end of the war was a good meal and they certainly got it at the Bottom Knockers and Cloggers Social Club that memorable night in rugby league history. The ale had run out and Ogdens had rushed an extra barrel over post haste on a hand cart. Their bellies full, the chairmen once more prepared themselves to listen to the tripe king's speech. This time he was to list the benefits for clubs who joined the Super League. Before he even opened his mouth he was met with a barrage of raspberries.

The proposals were as follows:

1. All clubs to receive £1000 to bring the grounds up to standard.
2. All changing rooms to have bidets fitted free by the sponsors.
3. Perfumed French soap to be provided.
4. The trainers' buckets to contain lavender water instead of cold tap water.
5. Urinating on the terraces to be banned. French toilets to be erected
6. The leading scorer in each club to receive free tripe and onions for a year.
7. The leading goal scorers and try scorers in the league to have a night out at the Follies Bergeres.
8. Brass bands to play on all grounds before matches.
9. All players and club officials in the Super League to receive sixpence off every meal they eat in a U.C.P. cafe.

10. All kit will be provided. Jerseys will bear the motif 'U.C.P. SUPER LEAGUE. KEEP FIT ON TRIPE AND ONIONS.'
11. Club pie shops to stock all U.C.P. products and the profits to go into club funds.
12. Free French lessons will be provided at night schools in every town. Conversely, English lessons will be provided in french towns.
13. Shopping trips twice a year to Paris for directors' wives. All expenses paid.
14. Pigeons to be replaced by telephones at all clubs.
15. Broadcasting rights to be negotiated with BBC and Paris Wireless and Telegraph Company. In compliance with the BBC rules all rugby league personalities who appear on the wireless must take a course of elocution lessons from a BBC announcer. All monies earned in this way will be pumped back into the Super League to the benefit of all clubs.
16. Each club to receive a free supply for the use of its trainer of Elliman's Rub and Alf Althorpe's Horse Liniment.
17. All season ticket holders to receive a bottle of french wine.

The mention of the thousand pounds had sent a thrill up the spines of all the chairmen and officials. It was unheard of money! Why, it was the sort of annual salary only a very prominent person in industry received. The business minds in the auditorium were adding, subtracting and generally calculating. There would be enough brass to do all the jobs and enough left over, 'appen,' to buy a good player. During this lull in the proceedings no one indulged in raspberry blowing. The minds of the 'men of brass' were working silently.

It took a brave man to stand there and listen to the insults and rude remarks. A lesser man would have fled. Deep in his heart and soul he realised that many of the proposals were quite preposterous to dyed in the wool men of rugby league. Instead of protesting at their ignorance he simply let the assembly have its head; he knew they would get it off their chests and settle down.

He knew his fellow northerners well did Seth. They could grumble like hell but if they could smell brass that would be the deciding factor. His patience bore dividends. Eventually the noise quietened down to few whispers and coughs. A couple of isolated raspberries blown by Ike Bilgebottom of Leigh threatened to start up the pandemonium again but with Joshuas help at last peace and quiet reigned. The chairmen were ready for the next earth shattering proposals.

The English sponsor then went on to explain that certain rules had to be adhered to and these were as follows:

1.   Players must not break wind in the scrum. All hookers to remove their false teeth.
2.   The Marseillaise to be played along with God Save the King at every match whether in England or France.
3.   All players to shave before matches and French soap to be used at all times in club baths.
4.   Referees to be bi-lingual.
5.   Croissants to be sold in the pie shops.
6.   No cloth caps allowed on French grounds. All travelling English spectators to wear French berets.
7.   All whippets and ferrets taken to France to be quarantined for 24 hours before the match.
8.   Washing of rugby balls in the bidets is not allowed.
9.   Clogs will not be allowed in the best stands, neither will whippets, ferrets and Uncle Joes mint balls.
10. French peripatetic onion sellers (unless franchised by the Super League) will be banned from all grounds and their bicycles confiscated.
11. If scent is used by players after the matches it must be Eau de Cologne, a subsidiary of the Chevalier empire.
12. Finally, all directors to wear plus-fours and spats at Super League meetings. Bicycle clips, flat caps and ratting jackets will be frowned on. The U.C.P. Super League intend to

impress the rest of the sporting world with its new sophisticated image. Spitoons in the best stands will not be tolerated.

Old Tommy Bottomley with the ear trumpet was the first to voice his opinion. Being deaf his voice was like a foghorn.

"I don't hold with queer Refs. Typically French, bi-sexual indeed! It's disgusting. We'll have hookers co-habiting in the scrums next". He crashed his ear trumpet on the table in emphasis.

"Someone clean his ear trumpet out – he's as deaf as a stone wall. We said *bi-lingual*! The referee will speak *both* languages" informed Joshua.

"Oh I see" said Tommy. "Lancashire and Yorkshire".

Jonah Hawksbody hammered on a beer crate. "This is no place for levity. Can we have your observations, gentlemen ?"

"You can have mine for nowt" shouted Bert Bradbottle. "If he thinks I'm wearing spats and all that tackle he's got another think coming. I've sat next to Lord Derby in the stand at Wembley wearing me cloth cap and goloshes with a bag of Uncle Joe's mint balls in me pocket. He's trying to make us go posh and it ain't on."

"I believe you wish to make a statement, Mr. Hepplethwaite ?" Jonah pointed a bony finger at the Bramfield man who was holding up his hand like a kid at school wanting a pee.

"I do indeed, Mr. Hawksbody. I refer to the rule no urinating on the grounds. Never let it be said that Joshua Hepplethwaite was a smutty man or given to sexual in your endos as my fellow chairmen will testify. But there are certain facts of life, basic though they may be, which we Northerners hold on to as our heritage so to speak. And one of 'em is enjoying a good slash on a rugby league ground. Creating little rivers in t'cinders, a pork pie in one hand and your John Thomas in t'other. After all, most lads are full of ale and need relief...."

"Did he play for Hull K.R. or St. Helens Recs"? It was old Bottomley again.

"Who?" snapped Joshua annoyed at the interruption.

"That Welsh lad, John Thomas." Joshua ignored the remark and continued his diatribe.

"You say we're to get French lavatories, Mr. Scragbottom, but I bet they'll stink just same as ours do on all the grounds. Let nature have its way, I say, and leave well alone."

"Hear hear" bellowed an unidentified voice. "I've seen 'em peeing in each others pockets in an emergency ".

"Cut that out! You're not at home tha' knows!" censored Hawksbody severely.

Mr. Scragbottom then announced the fixtures for the opening day:

Holyhead Hornets v. Bramley.

Dieppe Garlic and Shallot Co. v. Wigan St. Helens.

Dewslet v. Toulouse Tacklers.

Leeds Batley v. Paris Moulin Rouge Rovers.

Stanley Wires v. French Foreign Legion.

Barrowford v. Keighley.

Swinford v. London Chemicals

Yull v. Huddersfield.

Leigh Broughton v. Castleford.

Featherfax v. Holyhead Hornets.

Isle of Sark v. Brammersley.

Bradford Trotters v. Dunkirk Trinity.

When Mr. Scragbottom said "The League still has a certain familiarity about it gentlemen" he was greeted with a chorus of raspberries and boos.

It was well gone midnight when the meeting finally closed. The two Leeds directors who had come on a tandem had to be put up at the Bricklayer's Arms and others had to sleep in their cars. Before this it was a tired, yawning, bunch of chairmen who tried to keep awake as the tripe king gave his final address which ended as follows:

"....And so gentlemen, I hope you will agree to our proposals.

We assure you that your great game of rugby league will benefit a thousand fold. It may seem strange to you at first that french teams will be in the League. Do not forget that the French people will see it as strange also. We may be two different races but we have a lot in common. After all, we were on the same side in the war. Northern France and Northern England certainly have a lot in common. Coal mining, textiles, beer production and black puddings. European co-operation is a thing of the future. One day Europe will be one family..."

"Bollocks!" shouted Bob Halfpenny.

"I will ignore that ribald remark for now but remember gentlemen coarseness and vulgarity may have been part of rugby league in the past but it will not have a place in the new structure. Where was I? Oh yes . . . The next meeting of the Super League will be held a week on Thursday, two o'clock sharp at the new U.C.P. Restaurant next to Harrods in London. Goodnight gentlemen and thank you. I believe Mr. Hepplethwaite has a few more words to say". Joshua mopped his brow as he struggled to his weary feet.

"Just one last thing, lads. We've heard a lot of stuff tonight and we've had a jolly good argument for and against. We've got it off us chests and I ask you all to give every matter discussed your fullest attention and chew it over at your club committee meetings. Oh, and by the way, Mr. Chefsalleyway will be sending every club a typed memorandum in a french letter." As Joshua made his way to the door he met more opposition. An angry mob barred his way.

"Thanks for nowt Joshua owd lad!" Piped up Hadfield Barnacre who was spokesman for the rest.

"You've not heard the end of this. I'm going to issue a statement to the press about this business . . . . monkey business, I reckon as you're in this for financial gain – back hander was it?"

"If you put that in writing Hadfield I'll take thee for every bit 'o brass you've got lad!"

Hadfield gave him a vigorous V sign to which Joshua responded by blowing a loud raspberry before he sloped off into the cool night air to the Cock and Keyhole where he was putting up for the night.

The landlady, old Polly Bladderwart, took pity on Joshua and gave him a nip of brandy 'kept for medicinal reasons'. He was in such a bad state with the shock of the proceedings and his part as mediator that she filled up an old tin tub with warm water so he could have a good soak in front of the coal fire in his bedroom.

The soothing water and a bar of Lifeboy soap relieved him but he was sorely hurt at the remarks he had been forced to endure.

'What can't be cured must be endured' was a favourite remark of his poor old mother but why the hell did he have to take it on the chin? After all he'd only been doing his best. Some of those hard nosed directors had hearts of cold steel, they'd not made their money by being soft. Once in power they thought they could treat everybody else like muck. He'd heard all the stories about the way players were treated by directors at certain clubs. More like paid slaves than players and the directors like little Napoleons. At least he prided himself that Bramfield, his own club, wasn't run like that. They all got on well, players and officials, none of this summoned to the headmasters study as some old players used to call the committee room. No, he knew he couldn't expect praise and pretty talk from self made men like directors but he wasn't going to be walked on either.

Chapter 4

When he awoke the realisation of the previous days earth shattering statements sent him rushing for the chamber pot. Even the sight of three blue bottles swimming couldn't stop his eagerness for relief. The morning papers carried the amazing news of the Super League, which he read as he ate his dried eggs:

"PIGS TROTTERS TO SAVE THE LEAGUE" ran one headline, while a rival paper had "ANTI-FRENCH FEELING RIFE AT SUPER LEAGUE MEETING".

The jungle drums were rattling. The news rocked the north of England. Crowds gathered outside town halls to protest. Anti-French slogans were written on lavatory walls. Kilroy and Chad took a back seat to "Freddy the Frog".

The menace of Hitler had been put down. The normally passive people of Britain had opposed him in a dreadful anger when aroused. It was not in their nature to be aggressive. Yet, here they were, only a few weeks after the end of the war in Europe – most of the fighting forces not yet demobilised – gathering together in northern towns and villages to denounce a further injustice. They had dug for victory – rotting down piles of newspapers to provide manure for crops – treasured flower beds were given over to vegetables; village greens were dug up; bomb sites had been cleared and turned into allotments. They had suffered the trauma of queuing for hours on end at butchers' shops only to be given hardly enough meat to feed one man never mind a family. The Black Market had thrived and as always it was the poorer people who had suffered. Those with influence had the first choice. Versatility knew no bounds. Bananas were a thing of the past and yet go in the 'local' on Saturday night, (if you were lucky enough to find it open and beer available,) and you were sure to hear *'Yes we have no Bananas'* rattled cut on the old joanna. Folks laughed at their own misfortune, but it was hard to laugh at parsnips mixed with banana essence, dried eggs, potato sandwiches, tea that tasted more like scented dust and the never to be forgotten Snoek, a fish 'delicacy' in a tin.

Northern folks in particular have always loved onions. Tripe and onions was an institution and pickled onions were eaten by the ton. What most folks didn't realise was that the vast majority were imported, a very large amount from France. Onion sellers on 'sit up and beg' bicycles were a common sight. They would come over from France in droves to collect onions from wholesalers set up by the growers, collect supplies and set off round their stipulated areas to call on houses. As soon as the war started onions became very scarce and it was only when the 'Dig for Victory' campaign really took hold that stocks were replenished in 1944.

Many pages, dear reader, could be written on the hardships of war suffered by the people of Britain. So, I leave it to your imagination to picture the position in your minds. That institution, beloved by Lancastrians and 'tykes' alike, namely the Rugby Football League, was to be taken over and altered for ever. Featherstone and Batley lads had fought shoulder to shoulder in the war but they'd knock hell out of each other in peace time over rugby league and here was this bloody frog and his mate telling 'em to join forces! The very frog who had stopped sending onions over! Now he was wanting to flood the North with them and ruin their game in the bargain! Not bloody likely ! He was no better than Hitler, Mussolini, Goebells and all the rest of 'em! Sod that for a game 'o sowjers!'

Old Fred Fogg, the ferret king, managing director of *'Fogg's Ferrets of Featherstone'*, was a worried man. He was on the phone to Joshua at the mill only hours after he had read the paper.

"I've got a proposal, Joshua owd lad. Forget these onion fellers and go for my ferrets. Once they get in they'll try to muscle in on all our business – even yours. Stick to pure English sponsors. I'm afraid they'll bring French ferrets into England now the war's over so I'll put up some brass if you'll agree to call it Fogg's Ferrets Championship and put my advert on all jerseys."

Joshua listened out of politeness and promised to consider the matter. Ten minutes later Nat Dodd rang him. Nat was the North's biggest manure supplier and he wanted *'Dodd's for Dung'* on all jerseys. Each club would have their playing surface covered a foot deep in dung at the end of each season free of charge. He'd even give Joshua enough for his cabbage patch .

He decided to clear off for a while before the phone went again. His destination was the residence of Stanley Keighley the local undertaker and club scout. Stanley had been in the valleys scouting. By gum, they'd had some great Welsh men. 'Ee . . . he could reel 'em off like the two times table: Prosser, Owen, Tranter . . . but would they get any more? The war had played heck with a lot of chaps. Many of them had been wounded, some were too fatigued to play again, others just wanted to find a girl and get wed . . . yet there must be lots of lads who'd come North given the chance, a job and prospects. It was the signing on fee that was the killer. Some would even want £400. Nay, clubs couldn't do both. They couldn't satisfy safety standards at the grounds and pay out money like that to players who, after all, didn't always turn out to be good league men. Some just faded out and went home. Many were never given time to adjust.

The Super League money on offer was wonderful yet they'd almost have to sell their souls to get it. Hard headed business had no softness in its heart . . . but possibly at the London meeting some compromises could be suggested . . . all this was going on in Joshua's head as he walked up to Stanley's front door. He was tempted to walk straight in but thought better of it. Clara, Stanley's wife, was very unpredictable as Joshua had found to his cost on many occasions. So he hammered on the door with the cast iron replica of Jim Sullivan used as a door knocker. Clara, in a hair net and brown 'passion killer' stockings, gave him a dirty look when she opened the door. You would have thought she was opening the door to Himmler or Ribbentrop. She looked grumpy as a bag of tom cats.

"Oh, it's thee. Well don't stand there like tripe at fourpence. Come in. I were dusting the antimacassar and you fair gave me a start."

How the heck did Stanley ever get Clara for a wife Joshua thought as he sat on the sofa while she made a cup of tea in the scullery. Rumour had it he won her in a raffle. Booby prize of course. But despite all her queer ways she was a Bramfield supporter through and through.

"Ee, you look proper worn out, Mr. Hepplethwaite" she said as she poured the tea. "I suppose all this to-do over the new league is worrying you. I read it in the paper."

"It is, Clara, lass. I were on the podium all neet".

"Ee, I'm sorry . . . . 'appen it's a laxative you need. Have you tried centipedes?"

"Nay, it's not that, lass I mean the platform. I were the mediator between the U.C.P. and the R.L.F.C. and it were murder I can tell you. One of 'em called me Judus and another asked me where I was going to put me thirty pieces of silver. They think I'm selling 'em down the river. What do you think Clara, lass? You're a blunt lass so speak thee mind."

"I don't like the idea of joining up with Bruddersby. You might as well ask a Wiganer to subscribe to a Saint's benefit fund. Fancy them having to join together, an' all – it's fair turned things upside down. But I'm all excited about the French teams."

"Oh ? You do surprise me, Clara. Why's that?"

"Well, us ladies can do us shopping in the Champs Elijah and all them posh streets what they call bullyvoids. I'm sure your missus will want to go."

"Nay, Phoebe Maude would rather have a day out in Oldham. You'd only pay ten times more for a hat in Paris."

"Well I'm off if I gets the chance. I've often fancied frog's legs in asprin and I'd love to try them whore's duvets what they have before a meal."

Joshua was eager to get to business.

"Is Stanley in, luv?" As if in answer to the question the large frame of the Rovers' eccentric scout appeared in the kitchen doorway.

"How do, Mr. Hepplethwaite. What a bloody storm there's blowing up over this league". His wife, who never allowed swearing in her parlour, waved a bony fist at him.

"Cut that out, Stanley Keighley! Wash thee mouth out with that stuff the sponsors of Super League make."

"It's U.C.P. not T.C.P., lass!" snapped Joshua who was always on a short fuse when in the company of Clara Keighley. "Well, how did the scouting go in Wales Stanley lad? Any good."

"I watched a few games and I've approached a couple. Two of 'em fancy coming up for a trial if we'll pay their expenses. One's a forrard and the other's a full back. I met one lad who's very keen to come but he wants a guaranteed job. I felt sorry for him. He told me as how he came back to Wales on leave to find his wife had hopped it with a yank. Heart broken he was. I had to buy him a few beers to console him."

"Any excuse to drink strong liquors . . . my mother warned me about you and your fondness for the devil's juice. . . . ee but it must have been a shock for the lad. A proper hussy she must have been like that Jessy Bell in the Bible, They used to stone 'em you know."

"It's common, Clara, lass" said Joshua. "Lots of women went living over the brush and carrying on while their husbands were away. Some of 'em would do owt for chewing gum and nylons. If this chap's keen to come up give me his address and I'll send him a tenner for his train fare and digs and we'll have a look at him. And I want you to get round the local amateurs in the next few weeks and see if you can get ' em to play trials at Marl Heights. We've a lot of work to do Stanley if we want a decent side. We've got to get stuck in".

"But I thought we were joining up with Bruddersby?"

"Never, lad! As long as I've got wind in me lungs that'll never 'appen. Barnacre and me are both writing to 'em to object. We'll both join the Super League but not as one club. To think we just won t'war and here we are being told what to do!"

"There's some good points, though" insisted Clara. "I were reading all the rules and regulations in the Daily Dispatch. That bit about brass bands is a good 'un. There's nowt like music before a game. Up to now, we've only had it for cup-ties and such. My old Dad, bless his cotton socks, was leader of Bramfield Town Band and he loved music. He'd have been proud to have played at Marl Heights before Rovers matches. He'll be conducting some heavenly choir, no doubt ."

"Or 'appen a red hot jazz band" quipped Stanley.

"What do you mean!" roared Clara. "Just because he didn't like me marryin' you and him a leader of Temperance Union".

"Is that a brand of rugby union? I don't like either of 'em. One lot won't let you sup ale and the other lot are toffee nosed old farts who think it's great every time the ball's booted over the stand by the outhalf".

Clara ignored her husband's ribaldry-. "He brought us up to love music did my father. Cavalry Rusti-mechano, Verdi's Rectum, and all those areas from Carmen . . . *'He loves me not . . . He loves me not. . . de. de. de. . .d e. .dee deedle dee. . . He loves me not . . .de . . . de. . ."*

"Belt up lass! You've got a voice like a castrated stoat!" bawled

Stanley.

"I might tell you, Stanley Keighley, if you hadn't come on scene, I was going to be a metro-soprano. I'd love to have been a premier doner in opera like Nellie Melba, me dad were heart broken when I gave up singing lessons to marry thee".

"That's enough of that" said Joshua. "What do you think of us having matches broadcast on the wireless?"

"I reckon it's a belting idea" enthused the undertaker. If Rovers are away in France playing Dieppe Onion & Garlic Company we can listen in. Wireless was a great invention".

"Trust you to think of that .... you agree with all them new fangled things what pollute youth like picture palaces, dancing, and night clubs. That chap Macaroni what invented wireless might be a clever fellow but I don't trust foreigners. What if it blows up? It's alright for Tommy Handley and the news I reckon, but I don't hold much to it otherwise."

Clara chucked a bucket full of coke on the fire as if to emphasise her point.

"I reckon the french are reeking revenge on St. Helens for what they did to Napoleon", she continued as she blew up the fire with a pair of bellows.

"Yer what?" asked Josh.

"He were sent there when he were defeated. They've never forgotten it the French."

"*St. Helena* you crate egg – did they learn you nowt at that school you went to?" Joshua could stand no more of Clara's prattling and announced that he was going to leave. She was crying now.

"Ee I'm sorry, lass, if I upset you. Here, give your Uncle Joshua a big hug. Tell you what, how would you like a couple of meat coupons in return for some of Stanley's soap coupons. You could get yourself a bit of scrag end from t'butcher."

Her eyes lit up. "Thanks Mr. Hepplethwaite, I'd love to make some scrag end stew. It fair warms you up it does."

Stanley took Joshua into the coffin shop. It came as no surprise to the chairmen to see the ghoulish collections of dead men shoes, false teeth and other impedimenta left over in this world before their owners departed for the next one.

"You're a rum 'un Stanley. Making brass out of dead folk's belongings".

"It's only what they leave behind. The relatives leave it all to me. They don't like messing with dead bodies tha' knows. It's amazing how many have died with pockets full of soap coupons. Here's a couple – I reckon a quarter pound of scrag end is worth two."

"I tell thee what, Stanley, why don't you take a pile down to South Wales and use 'em for bait for union payers," joked the chairman.

"I will as long as committee recompense me."

"Don't do owt for nowt" said Joshua sarcastically.

"I won't lad," said Stanley seriously.

The Scout wasn't joking, either. It was well known he was one of the leading men in the local Black Market. The police could never catch him out but Joshua had often seen tins of John West salmon, canned fruit from Australia, and best butter in Clara's scullery. Although he had the chance Joshua had never dabbled in contraband food and petrol. Many a man had gone to prison over it. Rationing looked like going on for a good while. It would take the country a long while to get back to normality. He only hoped his scout didn't get caught. Bramfield needed him badly if they were to recruit fresh players.

Even though he was a 'crate egg' and given to doing daft things Stanley had an eye for a player just as he had a good eye for weighing up a corpse before he made the coffin.

It was imperative for a club to have a scout. One thing about Stanley, you could trust him – in matters of rugby league anyhow. In certain other matters Joshua would'nt have trusted him as far as he could have thrown him. Going by the undertakers ale belly that wouldn't be very far.

Some clubs employed free lance scouts who would work for anybody as long as there was a few bob in it. It was common knowledge that union players were often pestered by the same persistent scouts, week in week out on behalf of different clubs. One week the scout would be recruiting for Wigan, the next St. Helens, the next week Hunslet and each time the club in question would be the best in the league.

Not Stanley. He worked for Bramfield and no one else. He'd had many a scrape because of it too, a brawl or two in bars with other scouts after a few pints, not to mention the irate union officials who treated league scouts like vermin. Joshua chuckled to himself as he wafted the tea in his saucer with his bowler hat.

"What's in your mind Mr. Chairman? Penny for your thoughts," piped up Clara.

"Ee . . . . nowt luv. Simply thinking about club that's all. This is best tea I've supped since peace time lass. Did your Stanley get it?" The question went unanswered.

Having said his farewells to the Keighleys, Joshuas mind harked back over the years Stanley had been connected with his club Bramfield Rovers. It was strange but being an undertaker had been an advantage to Stanley, he could tell a chaps weight to within a couple of pounds by simply looking at him, a very useful acquisition in the armoury of an undertaker. So when he went to watch a R.U. man in a match he didn't need to be told his weight. Ee . . . we've had some adventures with him chuckled Joshua to himself! Secretly the chairman was fond of the scout even though he had almost driven him to drink at times. His main trouble was he was easily led especially when booze was concerned in the equation. The whole League knew about the incident when he signed a Welsh hooker with a wooden leg, then there were the times he'd dressed up in disguise to watch English R.U. men at fashionable clubs like

Wasps, Harlequins and Bath. Invariably he was spotted, usually given away by requesting pie and peas at the bar. Many a time outraged Union toffee nosed officials had set beagles on him. But Stanley had weathered the storms and at signing Welsh players he was the best in the whole League. No doubt he'd be up to his tricks again now the war was over, eager to get down to Wales boozing with those Welsh lads. Still, you couldn't blame him, being wed to Clara. She was hardly Marlene Dietrich.

He was surprised that she welcomed the Super League. He thought she would have condemned it out of hand but it was the lure of the Paris shops that attracted her. Good job his Pheobe Maud wasn't like that.

Little did Joshua realise that women would play a deciding part in the new adventure before them.

Effigy of Joshua Hepplethwaite being burned on Billinge Hill

Chapter 5

It was a week after Joshua's visit to the Keighley's and a most eventful week it had been too. The trip by the chairmen down to London had been undertaken and the idea of the new league was sinking in to all concerned although there were still many objections to the format. Joshua liked many aspects but in his heart of hearts he was a traditionalist and as he remarked to Phoebe Maude on his return from the 'big smoke' "I've a feeling in me water about it luv, it's like a dream really but I can't see it coming true."

This attitude was an irritation to his spouse who, as each day passed, was becoming more enchanted by the new league with all its grandiose connotations. It was O.K. being a chairman's wife but trips to Keighley and Hunslet were hardly on a par with trips abroad. In fact the only exciting trip was the journey to Widnes when the team and officials had a free ride on the old rattling transporter across the Mersey to Runcorn. Good old Widnes! It was hardly the home of Eau de Cologne with its fertiliser odours. They treated you right royally after the match but the lure of the venues in the new league put Widnes, Featherstone and the rest in the shade. She was sure she wasn't the only chairman's wife who had the same views.

She worried about Josh but she could see an improvement and

he wasn't complaining about his sphincter as much. Now the initial anger directed to him by the chairmen had subsided 'appen he'd be a happier chap. Little did she know that the anger felt by fans had not yet reached its peak despite the initial flare up.

Joshua was in good spirits as he flicked through the receipts in the petty cash till at the mill office. Miss Grimshaw had greeted him with some heartening news. Jimmy Jubb, a promising half back before the war, had arrived back from a prisoner of war camp and declared himself ready to play rugby again. Joshua was delighted.

"Eee, I'm sorry I missed him. Well, that's scrum half sorted out. Poor chap, he must have suffered, but I've heard other stories of fellows returning to clubs. One lad over at St. Helens, Jimmy Myers, a centre, was captured in 1940 and spent nearly all the war in a P.O.W. camp, then was forced to march up to fifty miles a day with only a bowl of soup and a piece of bread to sustain him. This was only a few months ago. He's home again and turned up at Knowsley Road in a pair of army goloshes to train! That's the spirit old England thrives on, Miss Grimshaw. Did you look after young Jimmy Jubb?"

"I made him a cup of Camp coffee and gave him some of those chocolate biscuits Mr. Keighley brought in."

"Good for you, Miss Grimshaw. It's wonderful to know that chaps like Jimmy after all they've been through are raring to go! Hey, but don't be mentioning biscuits and Stanley Keighley to anyone. Careless talk costs lives, remember. Think on".

"They're not really Black Market are they?" exclaimed Hyacinth aghast at the idea. "It's permissible to barter, surely? We simply swapped them for six eggs."

"Oh aye? But where did the biscuits come from in the first place? 'Appen they came down the Irwell on a banana boat and somehow landed up in a certain businessman's back yard . . . wink wink . . . cough cough . . . eh, Miss Grimshaw."

The naive secretary smiled but not being a woman of the world

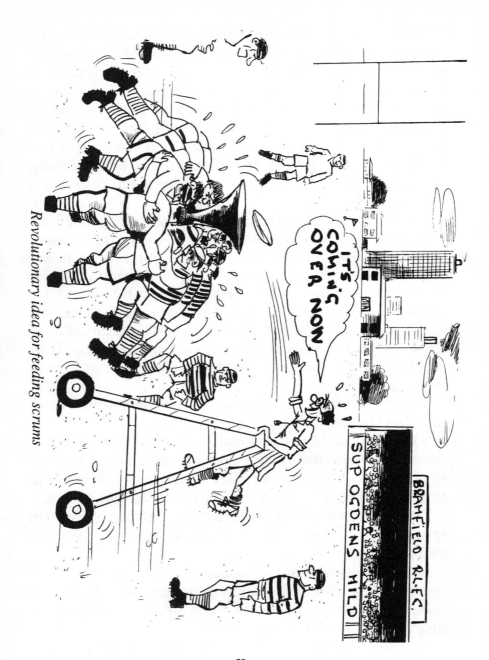

Revolutionary idea for feeding scrums

she shrugged off the very idea of Black Market transactions as she did the suggestions that some women actually went in pubs alone and (heaven forbid) some even lived with gentlemen out of wedlock. She was happy being as she was, the world could go its wicked way, she was content running the mill office and acting as Mr. Hepplethwaite's personal secretary for Bramfield Rovers, even though she had never been to a match. And now that the Super League was forming she felt certain she had a place on the administrative side. But surely Mr. Hepplethwaite wasn't referring to that nice Mr. Keighley – it was hard for her to accept that he was the leader of the Bramfield Black Market. Surely that pound box of Black Magic he'd given her for her birthday had been obtained legally by sweet coupons ? And those nylons? He said they were from a cousin in America – he must have a lot of cousins over there she mused. She knew at least six other women he had sold the nylons to. Spivs wore loud ties and trilby hats and spoke like Arthur English on the wireless. Dear old Mr. Keighley wasn't like that at all.

The arrival of the Daily Dispatch aroused her from her cogitative musing. "Have a decko at this, Miss Grimshaw," called out her employer. "It's about meeting we had in London with that French geezer."

Hyacinth had to swallow hard. Her boss's mode of speech sometimes grated in her head. Why do Northerners have to speak so gruffly and use bad grammar? Heaven forbid she was no snob but to compete in the international sporting world one would have to learn to project ones voice in a more cultured and correct manner. She for one was all for the new rule which stipulated that commentators on the wireless would be compelled to take elocution lessons from B.B.C. announcers.

"What does it have to say, Mr. Hepplethwaite?" she asked.

"Here, read it for yourself lass" said Josh handing her the paper.

The Dispatch had given a large spread to the London meeting:

"HISTORIC MEETING AT NEW   TRIPE SHOP. Yesterday

Cafe owner in Castleford ready for the French invasion

chairmen of the English Rugby League travelled to London for a meeting of the proposed new Super League. Hard nosed Northern business men often object to meetings held in London; they feel more at home in their environments of smoky industrial settings, but these men from Bradford, Batley, Widnes and all the other hot beds of traditional Rugby League activity travelled by special train to the hostile Metropolis. Were they greeted in cold clinical Southern style in an office more like a museum than a meeting place? Not a bit of it! The venue was the new tripe emporium at Harrods owned jointly by Messrs. Scragbottom and Chevalier, sponsors of the Super League. If I may be permitted to use Northern vernacular it was a reet gradely do – by gum not half!

But what of the business? It was the turn of Monsieur Chevalier to introduce French executives and chairmen to their English counterparts. As happened at the first meeting at Cleckheaton, much wrangling ensued but many of the Northerners were satisfied when the French sponsor agreed to pump extra money into club funds. A figure of £250 was finally agreed upon to supplement the amount already offered. Clearly, many chairmen found it hard to object to such monetary rewards. No matter what the implications of the new set up were. The question of amalgamation was a sore point for many but the sponsors put up an excellent argument in favour of clubs joining together.

One matter was agreed upon however. An international match will be held between the two countries to be played in Paris. This will serve as an introductory match for the new venture and hopefully whet the appetite for cross channel competition at league level. The organisation of teams could present a problem due to many players still being in the forces. The English chairmen took to the idea as a man and it was agreed that the team would be selected by Miss Hyacinth Grimshaw, an employee of Hepplethwaites Mills, Bramfield. Miss Grimshaw's task will be a difficult one, for many of the top players are scattered around the country in military camps."

English players promised onion franchises if they sign for French teams

"What do you think of that, Miss Grimshaw?"

"I feel very important, Mr. Hepplethwaite. Thank you for your confidence. I shall get down to the task this very afternoon."

And get down to the task she did with a vengeance. Numerous phone calls had to be made to clubs and military camps but after two days the woman who hoped her efforts would land her the job of official secretary of the Super League came up with the following British team:. Gus Risman (Salford), Johnny Lawrenson (Wigan), Jimmy Stott (Saints), Ernest Ward (Bradford), Roy Francis (Barrow), Ron Rylance (Wakefield), Tommy Bradshaw (Wigan), Ken Gee (Wigan), Joe Egan (Wigan) Frank Whitcombe (Bradford), Les White (York), Doug Phillips (Broughton), Ike Owens (Leeds.

"By the cram Miss Grimshaw I'm reet impressed!" enthused Joshua when he saw the completed team sheet.

"You've fair fettled it in gradeley fashion lass. A good mixture of young uns and old old heads, it's a team what'll hold its head up in any company. This won't go unnoticed lass. I'd be sorry to loose you love but if you did get taken on by the Super League as a secretary I wouldn't stand in your way."

"Oh thank you Mr. Hepplethwaite. Now shall we get down to the business of transport to France. There is the charabanc to hire and petrol coupons etc., to arrange. I'm told Mr. Stanley Keighley is to be team manager. The team will be in good hands then."

"'Appen so lass . . . but then again 'appen not."

Hyacinth placed a Du Maurier cigarette in her long holder and wondered what her employer meant.

Chapter 6

The very next day it seemed to the Bramfield chairman that all hell had been let loose in the press. The directors had got hold of several papers and were reading the reports over a pint in the Crab and Parrot in the town. Even the ale and Kearsley's pickle jar couldn't soothe Joshua's anxiety as he read the reports.

ST. HELEN'S NEWSPAPER. TUESDAY EDITION:

"Until recently the main topic of conversation amongst the men queuing for rationed goods (and in the public houses hoping for beer) has been the return of Saints players – Frank Tracy, Jack Waring, Jackie Bradbury and Jimmy Stott to mention a few. With the commencement of the Rugby League as we knew it prior to the war, naturally the old 'die hards' of Knowsley Road cannot wait to see peace time rugby again. Then what happened? As if to throw cold water on the hopes of our supporters two business men suddenly decided to take over the league lock stock and barrel for their own mercenary ends. Saints are to be amalgamated with Wigan! Rightly so the fans of both teams are up in arms. Have these people no souls? What place has money in sport? An angry mob protested outside the club house in Dunriding Lane on Tuesday night, a similar demonstration was held at Central Park. Effigies of Joshua Hepplethwaite, the Bramfield man involved in the new Super League, were burned on Billinge Hill the beauty spot equidistant from St. Helens and Wigan."

THE BRAMFIELD TRUMPET:

"Mr. Joshua Hepplethwaite, until recently a very popular figure

in the town as a prominent mill owner and Chairman of the Rovers, has suddenly become as hated as many of the monsters who perpetrated crimes in the war. Such a comparison would seem odious to a degree but I heard at first hand, vile accusations being bandied about in the Town Hall Square on Monday and I do not exaggerate. A large gathering of Bramfield supporters were vehemently protesting at the new Super League structure which links the Rovers with Bruddersby Stanley. Mr. Hepplethwaite, to his credit, it must be stated, tried to address the crowd. It took a brave man to stand before the angry supporters who chanted 'dictator' and 'Judas' as he attempted to address the crowd through a loud hailer. He might as well have attempted to hold back the waves at Blackpool. Extra police were rushed in to protect him. Stones were hurled and a stink bomb was thrown through his car window. When he returned home he found his bike tyres had been deflated."

NEWS OF THE WORLD:

"The Rugby League world is in turmoil. The new U.C.P. Super League is about as popular with supporters as Churchill is in Berlin. The man said to be at the centre of the storm is Joshua Hepplethwaite who claims he was simply acting as a mediator for the sponsors. Notwithstanding, he is carrying the can like it or not. Dog dirt was pushed through his letterbox and early yesterday whale innards and rotting horse meat were dumped outside his front door. When he visited Bramfield Hippodrome to hear George Formby, the celebrated entertainer, the booing lasted several minutes."

BRUDDERSBY STANDARD:

"Mr. Hadfield Barnacre, Chairman of Stanley, openly accused Bramfield Chairman, Joshua Hepplethwaite, of conspiring with

British R.L. team bound for France

business men to wreck the Rugby League for their own monetary ends. "Hepplethwaite is playing the innocent bystander, the mediator between the R.F.L. and the consortium involved in the takeover. I call him a snake in the grass. He is in it for his own ends. He has the gall to claim he doesn't want to see Stanley joined up with Rovers. What hypocrisy! This is part of his take over plan. He wants to rule over both clubs and oust myself and my directors. We have just put down one dictator. Are we to stand for another?" said Mr. Barnacre when interviewed at the club house on Tuesday."

Not all were anti Super League as this example shows:

LETTERS TO THE EDITOR – THE DEWSBURY CLARION & ADVERTISER:

"It is in the nature of beasts to prey upon one another. The spider entices the fly into its sinister web in order to devour it; the gazelle is mauled to death at the water hole by the marauding tiger; the fox stealthily stalks the hen run to kill for its food . . . Nearer home we see dogs chasing cats, ferrets killing rabbits – the world of nature is often a cruel one. These beasts are simply following an age old instinct. "But, what of human beings, I ask? Sometimes I feel they are just as base. The age old rivalry between rugby league fans often merges on mob rule and war. Let us put behind us these un-christian facets of our human behaviour. Now is the time to bury the hatchet. I welcome the new Super League and its proposed amalgamation of arch rivals such as Wigan and St. Helens. What an opportunity for christian charity to be put into action. Enemies of the past can become friends of the future. Full marks to the U.C.P.!"

The Rev. Dogsberry-Crockett. The Manse. St. Peters on the Hill."

Joshua thought "To hell with my water works, I'll give me kidneys a good swilling." Luckily for him the pub had just got a barrel on ration from Ogdens . All alone after the Kearsleys had departed 'owd Josh ' was almost crying into his ale. What the hell had he done? It was far from over however.

All that week letters, mostly against the league, appeared in the press and did little to cheer him up. Here is one from a far flung area:

THE SARK & CHANNEL ISLAND TRUMPET:

"Sir,
Through your pages I wish to express my horror and alarm at the introduction of Rugby League to the Isle of Sark.

Do the inhabitants of our tranquil isle realise that hordes of working class North of England folk will descend upon us ? I now paint a picture of the species: a drinker of copious pints of strong beer; given to belching in public and lewd songs; the consumption of fish and chips in newspapers and a broadness in speech encroaching on coarseness. Added to this many possess obnoxious dogs known as whippets and exhibit 'loud' braces in a manner liable to offend the sensitivities of the locals. Whilst I was prepared to tolerate the inclusion of league types in rugby teams during the war I am not prepared to allow such people to contaminate our lovely island in peace time .

> *Colonel Charles Pomfret-Carbody (Retired),*
> *Commander of Cavalry, Isle of Man.*
> *Ex-Hon.Sec. Old Bodleans R.U.*

The Hepplethwaites had very little respite. Even when they switched on the wireless they heard references to the 'upset in the north of England' caused by mill owner Mr. Joshua Hepplethwaite. Archive material was hard to track down after such a long time but eventually I did come across a cutting from a French newspaper:

"Monsieur Chevalier of Dieppe Onion and Garlic Co. R.L.F.C. is reported to have offered attractive terms to two outstanding Welsh players. They are Gus Risman, centre, and Alun Edwards,

Joshua leads out the makeshift British team in Paris much to the amazement of the referee

wing. *Both played for Salford Red Devils before they were disbanded on the outbreak of war. The terms offered are £10 per match win lose or draw and jobs as onion sellers for the company. Sponsored push bikes will also be given to the players if they sign. Both are said to be very interested."*

The following short piece is from a South of England paper.
"The Isle of Sark R.L.F.C. the new team in the Rugby Super League, are currently negotiating with Jim Sullivan, Wigan's legendary full back, to take up a post as coach. The have also offered him a job as harbour master."

Nearer home a Yorkshire paper carried the following letter:
Sir,
I, for one, do not share the pessimism and doom and gloom of the anti-brigade. The New League can only improve our beloved game. I am sure that I speak for all Rugby League aficionados when I say that next to the kicking duels between full backs (what pleasure I got from the five minutes long duels between Osbaldesten of Salford and 'Bunker' Carmichael of Bradford!) the most enjoyable aspect of the game is the scrummage, the more the merrier as they say. Yet, this gem in the crown of our game is often spoiled by the scrum half feeding his second row and, of course, 'feet up' by the hookers, and other dirty tricks these strikers of the ball get up to in the scrum. I have a plan which I hope the Super League will adopt. It will ensure fair and correct feeding of the scrum. A large pair of step ladders will be used by the referee who, upon climbing to the top, will deposit the ball down a funnel which will direct the ball to the hookers feet. I append a drawing of my idea.

> *Yours for the sake of our game,*
> *Archie Gumball, Featherstone.*

Over in France a restaurateur caused a storm of protest when he announced his plan to cater for North of England fans. A special menu of fried bread, dripping butties, pie and peas, steak puddings

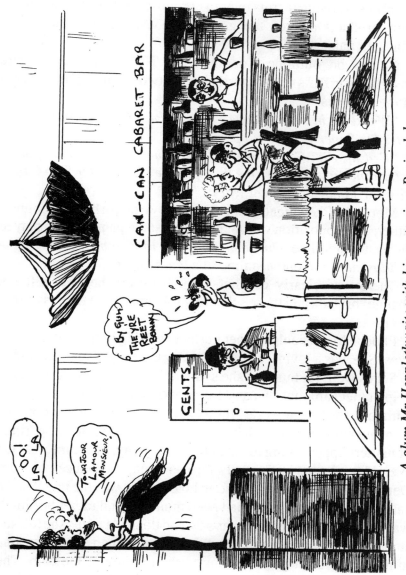

A glum Mr Hepplethwaite with his mates in a Paris club

and Yorkshire pudding would be on offer. Snails and frogs legs suppliers were up in arms over the proposal and threatened to sell their products outside the grounds to visiting supporters with educated palates.

Not to be outdone Yorkshire tourist entrepreneurs were advertising in Paris newspapers. Here are two examples I discovered in the archives:

"Weekends in Featherstone. Discover cultural Yorkshire. Special rates for Super League supporters."

"Fed up with Gay Paree? Visit Widnes the hub of England's entertainment scene. See the liners on the Manchester Ship Canal. Visit the famous chemical works."

Monsieur Chevalier did not escape the critics in his own country either. The opposition was mainly against the games being played in the summer time. *Only mad dogs and Englishmen go out in the midday sun!*, ran one headline in a Paris paper.

There was clearly conflict afoot between the 'we will not change' brigade and those scheming folk out to make 'brass' from the idea.

Phoebe Maud could see her husband wilting in front of her very eyes. She was a loving wife but there was a tough Northern streak in her as well. As much as she sympathised with him she couldn't help but feel anxious that any day he would withdraw his support. Although she had supported the Rovers since the very first time she went out with Joshua, back in 1922, she had only been on the fringe of matters appertaining to the club. Her big day, of course, was the Wembley victory in the early thirties, being introduced to Lord Derby and dining at posh London hotels. That was the icing on the cake which in many ways had been mundane and rather boring. It was a mans world when all was said and done. At times she felt she stood out like a sore thumb, she didn't know enough about the game to make any useful contribution to the running of the club. The Kearsley brothers, Joshuas co-directors, were nice enough blokes, but made it very clear that they didn't tolerate 'female interference'.

So, just like Hyacinth at the mill and that strange woman Clara Keighley she, too, had ambitions. All different but all three of them felt they had a place in the new sophisticated world of rugby league. Phoebe Mauds mental meanderings were interrupted by Joshua who had just come in after a pint at the Ferret and Foghorn. He was in a gloomy mood. He had considered the matter very carefully, he told her, and had decided to resign as Chairman of Bramfield. He would see the French match was held but afterwards he was going to pack in. This new Super League was too much of a worry. Phoebe Maud said very little but her mind was working like a shuttle in a cotton mill.

How often have we learned in literature how the best laid plans of mice and men are often brought to nothing by the wiles of women. In Mrs. Hepplethwaite's mind Joshua's waterworks problems brought on by all the worry were secondary to thoughts of shopping trips to Paris and the promised holidays in the South of France.

Unknown to her husband she contacted Hester Blanche Barnacre and was greeted in a surprisingly cordial manner. The two women had never met but the animosity their husband's showed to each other was not shared by the wives. Far from it, Hester Blanche was determined Bruddersby would join the Super League even if it did mean linking up with Bramfield. Hadn't women suffered enough in the war? And it was no better now peace in Europe had been declared. Food was still rationed and clothes were only obtainable by coupons. It was going to be a long time before things were back to normal. Why should the women miss out on trips to France with the teams? And those shopping trips to Paris . . . well, who in their right mind was going to miss them? Holidaying in the South of France . . . why, Hadfield took her to New Brighton for a week every year and that was it. And here he was saying he'd rather join up with the devil than amalgamate with Bramfield. He'd jolly well have to sink his pride! She'd see to that!

So this formidable duo of females decided upon a plan. Hester

Blanche would organise the Yorkshire ladies and Phoebe Maud the Lancastrians.

Joshua thought his wife was going for a shopping trip to Manchester. Little did he know that she was chairing a meeting at the famous Midland Hotel. Hester Blanche was doing the same at a hotel in Leeds. Both meetings reached the same conclusion. Their husbands joined the Super League with all its implications or the wives would withdraw wifely duties and favours : -

1. No cooking until they signed up with U.C.P.
2. All dishes to be left in the sink for the men to wash.
3. They would forego butchers meat and buy whale meat instead.

If these measures failed then other rights would be withdrawn. As this was discussed in whispers and nods I have no way of knowing exactly what was meant, but Clara Keighley was heard to remark later on that the ladies would 'withdraw conjugations'.

It was a downtrodden gaggle of beaten men who gathered at the Bat and Bulldog in Halifax only four days after the ultimatum delivered by the ladies. This assembly of giants of industry – business directors, mill owners and manufacturers were like chastened school kids. Gone was their aplomb and arrogance well known to business rivals and employees and to players too.

To a man they agreed to the Super League in all its forms. Even Joshua and Hadfield shook hands on the formation of their new club. Saints chairman took a large swig of his brandy and forced himself to shake hands with his counterpart in Wigan.

"Never trust a bloody woman" was a remark echoed by all hands.

Mr. Scragbottom had won hands down. What a move it had been when he had given Mrs. H. those chocolate biscuits! Get the women on your side and you can take over the world.

Seth was a very happy man as he set off for France to watch the historic match which would herald in the new league. A new era was dawning!

Chapter 7

If someone had gone round Bramfield shouting 'plague', the women folk's couldn't have moved any quicker. As old Ma Potter remarked to her pal in the bread queue "I saw owd Nelly Sprocket running like Stan Brogden down touch line at Marl Heights."

Why was she in such haste? Little Polly McHugh had got bananas in her greengrocer's shop in Bucket Street. Bananas! In next to no time a queue had formed from Polly's shop a hundred yards long into Gasworks Terrace and on to the canal bridge.

Some wit started up with *'Yes we have no Bananas'* but this was countered by the popular Tommy Handley song *'Bananas are coming back again'* a great favourite with wind up gramophone devotees.

News spreads like fire when women are in a queue. A banana boat had actually landed at Preston Dock, the first one for four years. Fruiterers from all over Lancashire had descended on the port in the early hours of the morning. It was like a ray of warm sunshine on a cold winter's day. 'Appen stuff like imported tin fruit and fresh pineapple would appear once again.

Clara Keighley was one of the fortunate ones. She got her three bananas before the supply ran out. "Ee, it's like old times Clara lass" she said to herself as she walked down a cobbled snicket on the canal bank where there was a wooden seat facing a stagnant stretch of water full of old prams, dead cats and tin cans.

Peeling the prized object with the reverence befitting such an occasion she heaved a sigh of contentment as she sunk her false top set into the luscious fruit. What a delight! Even her Stanley hadn't been able to produce bananas. Just then the sun broke through the dark clouds to cheer her up no end. The future was looking very rosy. The war was over in Europe and strong rumours that the war in Japan was almost finished. Soldiers returning from the battlefields, young lads returning as young men. Ee, it was nice to see them again.

To make matters even better in a month or so rugby would be starting up again at Marl Heights. She had heard through her husband that it was proposed by the sponsors to commence the league in the winter for the time being then to move on to summer rugby. It had always rankled with Clara that Stanley had never been made a director of Rovers. She could sit in the directors' box if that happened alongside Mrs. Hepplethwaite. The chairman's wife was nice enough but Clara always felt she was that bit superior. After all she was a mill owner's missus. It was a case of 'nice to see you Mrs. Keighley' and 'same to you Mrs. Hepplethwaite'. Distant but polite conversation when ever they met in the best stand. 'Appen that would all change with the Super League. She had aspirations to lead the singing before the home games. She'd already fixed it with the leader of the brass band, so that was a feather in her cap for a kick-off. If only Stanley was a more stable character. Trouble was the directors looked upon him as a bit of a clown. Even though he had found the club lots of good welsh lads he had never lived down the blunder he made in the 'thirties when he had signed a Welsh hooker with a wooden leg. Drink, that was the problem, and she knew in her heart that he would have to alter his ways if he wanted to get on in the club now the Super League had come. She'd even suggested electrocution lessons to make him speak proper but he wouldn't agree. Still, she mused, a new world is opening up both in ordinary life and in sport. She was determined to be a leading light in the future despite her Stanley.

That evening back at No. 6 Arkwright Sidings she was warbling a popular song of wartime *'I don't know what to do with me*

Gasmask' and accompanying herself with a couple of soup spoons on an upturned saucepan. She had just returned from another stint queuing for whalemeat at Claude Osmotherley's knackers yard. Not being on the ration you could buy as much as you wanted.

"Ee, it were funny, luv" she said to her husband who was polishing up a couple of brass handles for a coffin. "Owd Dolly Bagshott was in front of me in't queue and she says to Claude 'Give us two pound of whalemeat Claude and I'll have the head for the cat'".

Stanley didn't laugh. He had other matters on his mind.

"You better make me sandwiches, Clara. I'll need a lot if we're going all the way to France."

"What do you want, whalemeat or spam?"

"Don't talk rubbish. I've a nice bit of ham on the bone in that bag. And don't be giving the bone to a dog or folks will be wanting to know where it got it from. Think on, you've got to box clever."

Clara didn't ask questions. Stanley was a genius at supplementing the rations. She didn't even think about it. She couldn't understand how both of them had put weight on during the war. It was middle age spread she told her neighbours. Nothing to do with food of course. Dutifully she made up her husbands sandwiches.

"Do you reckon as they've chamber pots in France, Stanley lad?" She asked.

"They invented 'em, didn't they? Why do you ask?"

"What if you're taken short? I'd take your A.R.P. warden's metal helmet if I were you. You can urbanate in that if you're stuck. What's the arrangement about travelling then? Is Mr. Hepplethwaite getting a chara?"

"We can't get petrol, lass, so I've hired one of Bob Butterworth's coal wagons".

"Coat wagons? Are yer going soft in yer yed? What are the players going to sit on?"

"Coffins, lass. They're as comfy as owt else. We've got one in t'parlour haven't we? You never complained about it."

"Aye, but we've got cushions on it".

"We're talking about rugby league players, Clara. Tough chaps, they're not bothered about hard seats."

"How the hell are they going to play rugby after travelling in a coal wagon? Are you sure you can't get a chara?"

"I tell thee we can't get petrol. Have you got cloth ears or summat?"

Clara was nothing if not persistent.

"How is you can get petrol for one of Bob Butterworth's wagons and not for a chara?"

"Because Bob's got plenty, that's why."

"Can't the league buy it off him and send team in a chara? I'm going to ring up Mr. Hepplethwaite. I don't like thee travelling to them foreign parts in an open coal truck."

"I'm driving, lass. I'll be dry as a stick so don't thee fret."

"What are you up to, Stanley lad? Why can't you hire Bob to drive his own wagon? And where's Mr. Hepplethwaite going to sit? Is he in cab with you?"

"Nay lass, he's going separate with a gang of supporters and ex players. They're going on the train to Dover. In fact, they're on the way now. And keep thee nose out of it, Clara lass, you might be boss in this house but I'm in charge of the team. Mr. Hepplethwaite and his secretary said so."

"Oh, that painted posh piece what he's got. Talks with a plum in her gob and smokes fags in a holder. She's peas above sticks, she is. I've heard about you getting her nylons and chocolates. You're taking her to Paris aren't you?"

"What, in a wagon? Coals to Newcastle?"

"And what do you mean by that remark? Oh, I know. Paris is full of them destitutes in cafes and women soliloquizing on them bullyvards. That's what you mean isn't it? Them women have Venetian disease, don't come back here if you get that. Think on!"

"Cut it out, Clara lass. What's for tea? I want a good tuck in. I'm meeting team in Bramfield Town Square at 9 o'clock. We're travelling by night."

"Why not in early morning?"

"Will you stop asking questions and get me ruddy tea! What are we having?"

"Well, seeing as I'm using up that ham shank for your sandwiches it's a choice between bacon and nettles and whalemeat pie with paradise pudding to follow. You can have a bowl of allotment soup to start with. I put a nob of margarine in the soup to give it body."

"What the heck is paradise pudding, any road up?"

"It's made with dried eggs, it's vicar's favourite. I'm saving him a dish full. He likes my cooking does the vicar."

"You can give him whole ruddy lot, luv, for me. I can't stand dried eggs. And don't be giving me them nasturtium sandwiches again, lass. They learn you some funny things at that women's institute you go to."

"I reckon as I've done well with make do and mend on food front. I've dug for victory I have and invented all kinds of foods to eke out. carrot Christmas pudding, curried rabbit, sweet potato pudding, rose hip tart . . . ee I've been a good provider, Stanley."

"Appen so, but what about me? What about the little 'extras' I've got us? How would you have done if you didn't have a husband in the 'know', eh?"

"I don't want to know about your little deals, luv . . . here, get stuck into the allotment soup and you can polish off remains of the whale meat."

After tea Clara decided Stanley needed educating. She was most concerned about her husband's lack of knowledge about France. If the Super League was to take off then he would need to go over there scouting as interchange of players would be allowed. She'd feel proud of him. He'd be a sort of international celebrity would Stanley. 'Appen she'd go with him – she'd love a new hat. But it was no use, he'd have to parley French language or they wouldn't understand him. But he was stubborn was Stan. He'd said to her when she'd broached the subject of lessons "Why should I learn their lingo? We're on the mainland, they should learn ours".

He'd show her up, she knew it. That's why she had taken out a library book all about France. "I'm going to ask you some questions, luv. I don't want you going there being ignorant. Here's a good 'un. It's one o' them cultural questions: *Who painted the Mona Lisa?*"

"That's easy" answered Stanley. "Camel Lairds. They do all the Isle of Man boats. It's time I were getting doing. I've a lot of coffins to get out, Clara lass".

"I'll give you a lift if you like, luv".

"Nay, Clara lass. You sit by t'fire – I'll chuck some more coke on and I'll make thee a cup o' tea . . . don't worry about me lass . . . sit where you are and enjoy yourself looking at your wartime cookery book." He even gave her a kiss on the forehead.

What's got into him? Clara could smell a rat. 'Appen that posh bit off stuff was going after all? Still it was nice to be waited on for once so she stayed put by the fire. 'Appen she'd find out if he was taking her, it would all come out in the wash.

An hour later old Bob Butterworth brought his coal wagon round the back to the coffin shop for loading. "I've a bag of slack Stanley owd pal. I'll swop thee for a couple of clothes coupons. I'm sure you've got plenty knowing thee."

"I have but its all above board Bob."

"Ee . . . of course lad. I never thought otherwise" said the coal man giving Stanley a wink.

"What the hell is in those coffins, Stanley? Some of 'em are bloody heavy. You have emptied 'em haven't you? I don't want to be involved with corpses and all that Burke and Hare stuff, lad. I sometimes think you're twopence short of a full shilling" Stanley ignored the remark. At last the wagon was ready and the undertaker drove off to meet Miss Grimshaw who had organised the players to meet in the Town Hall Square. 'Ee, she wasn't bad looking at all. 'Appen he would ask her out sometime. Pity she didn't speak proper.

All the players turned up, some in army and R.A.F. uniforms. 'Ward's Wizards' were not in the least put out by the mode of transport. They had had five years of travelling in service trucks and wagons. They were simply glad to be off on a footballing trip. All of them to a man couldn't wait to get their boots on again in a game of rugby league. It was a very jolly party of footballers who set off on the epic trip to France. 'Wards Wizards' captained by that great centre Ernest Ward were as happy as a party of schoolboys despite the hardness of the seats and the smoke stack on the wagon which constantly emitted a fall of soot. Inside the cab Stanley munched on a ham sandwich and grinned like a Cheshire cat. Everything was going according to plan.

Chapter 8

Joshua sat in the changing room at the Paris stadium in a disconsolate mood. "Where the bloody hell are they?" he kept repeating. With only half an hour to go before the game Stanley and the British team hadn't turned up. "I should have me yed tested for letting him drive the players. He'll be in some ruddy scrape or other." "What do you expect Joshua owd prater? He did sign a chap what had a wooden leg." This jibe by one of the chairmans boozing pals for once fell on stony ground. The minutes were ticking by and the atmosphere in the changing room was charged with tension. Joshua could have willingly throttled his scout. "As if I haven't had enough blooming worry lately. Accused of this, accused of that, villain oft' bloody piece, it's been open season for declaring war on Joshua Hepplethwaite and now this! Still it's par for t'ruddy course with Stanley, he always does everything arse about face. "I'll swing for yon mon one day".

Added to all Joshuas troubles the journey to Paris had been a nightmare. The charabanc had broken down near Crewe so Joshua and his mates had to thumb lifts to the famous railway junction. Giving lifts to strangers during the hostilities had been frowned upon by the government due to the movement of German spies around the country. The lack of cars due to the acute petrol shortage had made matters even worse so it was several hours before the party got together at Crewe. They were tired and hungry, the grub in the refreshment room was extremely basic and the sight of a tea lady dusting the sandwiches didn't help matters. After a three hour wait they boarded an antiquated train for London. Packed together like sardines in compartments without a corridor or toilet facilities. After bellyfulls of saccharined tea it was an agonising trip. They were dying for a slash as the saying goes.

"There's only one thing for it" Joshua had said, "When we go into a tunnel open windows on both sides and get peeing. The longer the tunnel the longer the pee." To make matters worse the boat trip was very rough and the train to Paris had stopped at every station and halt on the way. So it was no wonder the party were worn out.

Little did they realise that the vast majority of them would get very little rest that afternoon in the cauldron of the roasting Paris stadium.

With ten minutes to kick off Joshua reached panic stations. French officials were rushing hither and thither uttering incomprehensible words and throwing up their arms as is the wont of foreigners.

"There's only one thing for it" Joshua told the referee who was gesticulating like a mad man and gabbling away in French. "Me and the lads will have to turn out. I'll go and ger 'em out of best stand". Many of them were ex players and not one of them was under forty. After a lot of argy-bargy and swearing twelve of the party were press ganged into turning out. The air was blue with Northern invectives.

Fortunately playing kits were available but the elastic in many of the shorts wouldn't stretch far enough to accommodate the beer bellies. At last, twenty minutes after the proposed kick off time, the makeshift British team were ready to go on the field. Joshua looked over his men. If the situation had been different Bramfields chairman would have burst out laughing. The sight before him reminded him of a clown act at Blackpool Tower Circus. Such a motley lot had never assembled in a changing room before or since.

"We're a sorry looking lot and I include myself in that statement. But, remember lads, we're doing this for the mother country. Clench your teeth and think of England! And remember, lads, play like gentlemen and make it a clean game, but if anyone gets hurt make sure it's one of them. For England and St. George!"

With that war cry on his lips Bramfield's intrepid chairman led his men down the tunnel into the stadium. Christians into the lions den. Cannon fodder. Innocents for slaughter.

It would be very unfair of me to reveal exactly what took place on that field, for to do so would be to discredit British sport. The thirteen conscripted men were like chaff before the scythe. Like the horsemen in the infamous charge of the light brigade they had been doomed before they began

Bravery was the one factor which shone forth, although many of the stand-in team were ex-players they hadn't played for several seasons, while the rest were a mixture of men who had, at one time, played amateur rugby and others who had never played at all.

The only time they came near to scoring was when Joshua, more by good luck than good judgement, picked up a loose ball by the French try line. He was hoisted aloft by his mates and used as a battering ram to bore a way through the French pack. Unfortunately his top set fell out of his mouth which caused one of his mates to loose his footing when he stood on them. Down went the lot of them like a pack of cards.

In the changing room after the match Jonah Hawksbody was furious at the non arrival of the British players and his anger was directed at Joshua who carried the can for everything.

"There will be a full investigation, Hepplethwaite, your man Keighley will be held responsible and so will your club. What happened today was a disgrace, the British Rugby League has been made a laughing stock."

The speech was received by a chorus of raspberries from the sweating deputies and the official wisely left before he was thrown into the bath. The only consolation of the whole trip was a night out at the Follies Bergeres but most of the party were so tired they kept falling asleep despite the attraction of the dancing girls and the lively music. Even the exotic can can did little to excite them.

"If they had decent ale I wouldn't mind" remarked Joshua as he sipped his wine." "If they expect Northerners to come over here to watch rugby league they should get some decent English ale in. They may be experts on frogs legs and champagne but if they don't get some decent booze for t'lads from Bramley and Widnes to sup they're on a loser from t'start. I'll bring that point up at next meeting of Super League Committee. This stuffs like gnats piss." The chairmans speech was greeted with yawns of approval, his mates were too weary to speak. As every northerner worth his salt knows there is nothing like a few pints of good northern ale to revive a chap. Not that southern slutch they serve up in posh R.U.club bars, but reet gradely brews from the likes of Sam and John Smith, Boddingtons and John Willie Lees. To add insult to injury our heroes, who had battled so bravly, were forced to sup wine which had probably been watered down and forced to pay through the nose for it.

There was only one thing for it and that was to get some kip. Before that Joshua was in for quite a surprise.

Casting his eyes around the night club he was attracted to a familiar looking chap wearing an atrocious wig. Two scantily clad girls were fawning over him and drinking wine out of slippers. All of a sudden Joshua recognised him. "Well, I'll go to our house! Would you ruddy well believe it! Ee but this beats cock fighting!"

He flagged the photographer over and requested that he take a picture of the man with the girls. As the camera clicked one of the girls was sitting on his knee.

"Ee, that'll do reet champion" enthused Joshua handing over some francs. "You never know when these things come in useful. Thought he'd wear a wig did he the crafty sod! I'd recognise yon mon dressed in armour."

So without more ado Joshua led his weary pals away from the high life of Gay Paree to seek much needed sleep. Even in his dreams the face of Stanley Keighley kept appearing, as is the way of dreams bizarre and weird permutations flashed into his sleeping mind. Stanley had done a deal with the Isle of Sark, the new club in the Super League, and sold the entire British team to the club. Instead of heading for Paris in the wagon he had gone to a port, and taken a ship to Sark. Boiling in oil; roasting over a fire; kicked in

the backside for half an hour every day for a year by Jim Sullivan
... all these extreme punishments presented themselves to him in
his dreams which reached nightmare proportions when Stanley
was hanged by his private parts from the goal posts when Sark
visited Marl Heights to play the Rovers.

It is little wonder, dear reader, that Bramfields much maligned
chairman woke up in a grotty Paris garret in a foul mood. 'Breakfast'
of dry rolls and thick black coffee did not improve his temper.

His "ast geet no black puddings missus?" fell on deaf ears. Little
did our Josh know that those succulent products of Bury were
going to play an important part in the on going saga of the Super
League.

Chapter 9

As Joshua walked up the cinder path to the Keighley's house, his ears were jarred by the strident notes of a harmonium being played out of tune.

"Oh, bloody hell, she's at it again" said Joshua to himself. He was on a very short fuse, tired out after a horrendous journey from France. Due to the huge number of British troops homeward bound from european warfields the ships were packed and the train schedule in England had been completely devastated. Joshua had been stranded at Crewe for ten hours. Here he was on the Thursday morning back in Bramfield after leaving Paris on the Sunday. So it was little wonder that Clara Keighley's disjointed harmony aggravated his torn nerves. Stuffed in his pocket was a french newspaper which had been sent over by special courier to the mill office. He had come straight to the house after collecting it from the postman.

The noise was so loud that it took Clara several minutes before she heard his knocking. Joshuas mutterings would have shamed a bargee. "You'll wake the dead, lass" he said when eventually ushered into the parlour.

"Ee, you're just in time, Mr. Hepplethwaite. I were just practising. I've been given the job of leading the community singing at Marl

Heights when the Super League starts. Listen to this."

Before Joshua could stop her she shattered his eardrums yet again, this time with her voice:

"A word allow me! Sweet ladies and gentlemen
I pray you hear why alone I appear.
I am the Prologue!
Our author loves the custom of a prologue to his story.
And as he would revive for you the ancient glory
He sends me to speak before ye.
But not to prate as once of old,
That his sighs and cries and the pain that is told,
He has no heart to feel
No, no! Our author tonight a chapter will borrow
From life with its laughter and sorrow.
Is not the actor a man with a heart like you?
So 'tis for men that our author has written
And the story he tells you is true!

A song of tender mem'ries
Deep in his listening heart one day was ringing
And then with trembling heart
He wrote it and he marked the time with sighs and tears.
Come then. Here on the stage you shall behold us in human fashion
And see the sad fruits of love and passion.
Hearts that weep and languish
Cries of rage and anguish
And bitter laughter!

Ah think then sweet people
When ye look on us clad in our motley and tinsel;
Ours are human hearts beating with passion.
We are but men like you, for gladness or sorrow,
'Tis the same broad heaven before us

The same wide lonely world before us
Will ye hear then the story?
How it unfolds itself surely and certain?
Come then, ring up the curtain!

"That's enough, lass" bellowed Joshua. "What the hell is it, anyway? It sounds like the tune the old cow died of. You can't sing that at a match! It'll put the mockers on the Rovers, will that".

"That's the Prologue to Pally Archie that is. It's class stuff is that."

"I don't care how pally Archie is but you want sing-song stuff before a match. White Cliffs of Dover, Hey little Hen lay me an Egg for my Tea, Hang out the Washing on the Siegfried Line and all them, that's the stuff the speccies want to join in, not blooming opera."

"I don't agree Mr. Hepplethwaite. When we go into the Super League we'll be up market. It's a new era lad . . . sophisticated, that's the word isn't it?"

"It is lass and you've got it right for once."

"What did you say?"

"Nowt, lass".

"We've got to look forward and mix with new people and we'll do that if we spread the game. I'm all for the new league, it can't spread far enough for me. The world is our Ostrich. I'm longing for the day when Russia joins in and then we can go sailing up the Vodka. Leading the singing is only the first step for me. I intend to go far in this new league. Me and my Stanley have plans."

"Now before you go any further lass I think I better tell you . . ."

"Ee, it'll wait lad. 'Appen it were a bit doleful that aria. Tell you what, how about this? It's one of Gracie's songs. They used to call me the Bramfield Nightingale when I were younger."

"More like a crow" muttered Joshua fidgeting with his bowler hat.

"Yer what?"

"I said *I know".*

"Get a lug 'ole full of this . . . hang on, I'll just pump up the harmonium with me foot . . . . that's better". In a voice that would have stripped wallpaper she began:

"Walter and me we've been courtin' for years
But he's never asked me to wed.
When leap year comes round I'll give three hearty cheers
Hip hip hooray, Hip hip hooray, Hip hip hooray!
Then I'll do the asking instead.
I don't want to die an old maid
So I'll sing him this serenade . . . .
Walter, Walter, lead me to the altar
I'll make a better man of you
Walter, Walter, buy the bricks and mortar
And we'll built a love nest for two.
My bottom drawer's all packed and ready
My bridal gown's as good as new,
Walter, Walter, lead me to the altar
And make all me nightmares come true!

"Walter, Walter, lead me to the altar
I don't cost must to keep in food
Walter, Walter, mother says you ought to
So take me while she's in the mood.
You know I'm very fond of chicken
We'll raise a lovely little brood
Walter, Walter, lead me to the altar
And I'll show you where I'm tattooed!

"Walter, Walter lead me to the altar
Don't say I've met me Waterloo
Walter, Walter tears make me falter
And I've lost me handkerchief too . . . .

Don't muck the goods about no longer
My old age pension's nearly due
Walter, Walter, lead me to the altar
It's either the work house or you!"
Joshua clapped politely.

"Ee, you enjoyed that Mr. Hepplethwaite didn't you . . . . 'appen I will sing 'em a few funny 'uns as well as the class songs. If my Stanley becomes a director of the Rovers . . . ."

"Hang on lass!" Joshua had to shout to make an impression. "There's no chance of that, lass, not for a long time anyhow."

"Aren't we good enough for you, then? After all my Stanley's done for the club. What about all them Welsh lads he signed? Just because I don't talk posh. . ."

"Nay, it's nowt to do with it. I tried to tell you but you would sing. I've some bad news, Clara lass. Your Stanley is in lumber in France. He's in clink. Prison lass".

"Yer what! Spoiling all my dreams, all my plans for a better life. Gone off with one of them profligate tarts I reckon. Me mother said he were no good. I could've wed a chirrypodolist you know . . . good practice he has an' all, doing all posh folk's feet in Cheshire . . . and what will the vicar say?"

"Nay lass, it's nowt to do with women or booze".

"That's a change! What else is there?"

"Smuggling. Contraband running, caught by the customs he was, red handed."

"Ecky Thump! What were he smuggling? Dirty books I bet. Trust him! Mucky devil!"

"Nay, nowt to do with that stuff. Black puddings. Black Market ones from Bury."

"You're 'aving me on, Mr. Chairman!"

"No Clara lass. That would be cruel. I'm deadly serious lass. Honest. Your husband may be a blundering old sod at times, beggin' your pardon, Clara, but beneath the bumbling facade there's a clever brain. He's the Professor Moriarty of the Black

Market . . . don't tell me you never suspected?"

Her face blushed so much that Joshua thought she was going to explode.

"Go on, tell me more" she managed to croak at last.

"Well, all that talk about him not being able to get petrol coupons for the charabanc was all baloney and balderdash. He didn't want to go on a chara, didn't suit his plans. So he hires a wagon and puts seats in ..."

"He used his own coffins . . . I can swear to that . . . ."

"Oh aye . . . course he did . . . and fills 'em up with black puddings for France".

"But who was he selling 'em to? He can't speak french."

"There's a way round every thing lass. Behind all us backs what does the slimy beggar do? Why, he gets hold of Monsewer Chefsalleyways phone number and rings him up . . . How's that for skullduggery!"

"Well I never!" Clara's false teeth were rattling with shock.

"Fixed up a deal they did . . . it seems black puddings are a delicacy in posh Paris restaurants and with the war over there's a rush on to get decent grub to sell."

"You mean that chap what's sponsoring the new league along with the U.C.P. chap?"

"The very same, Clara. But I'd better read you this article from France – Soir, a Paris paper. I got it sent post haste from France:

SMUGGLING SENSATION!
BLACK PUDDINGS ROCK THE SUPER LEAGUE

Gendamerie patrolling a busy road fifty kilometres from Paris stopped a wagon carrying an English registration. It was purely a precautionary check but it turned out that it was the means to an end in arresting notorious racketeers – in particular the "black hand" who reigned as the Arch Supremo of the contraband world before the war. The wagon contained the British Rugby League

Team bound for Paris to play a French Select 13 as a curtain raiser to the new Super League. The driver, Mr. Stanley Keighley, undertaker and scout for an English club, satisfied the gendarme that his papers were in order. Only for a blunder on his behalf, the wagon would have passed the inspection. When Mr. Keighley asked the gendarme if he was on the right road to Paris the officer replied "Oui Oui". Mr. Keighley took it as a request for the players to urinate before continuing the journey. When the players had left the wagon the gendarme was curious to know what was in the coffins the British players were using for seats. Told that they contained only jerseys and boots, etc., he investigated further to find six hundred weight of black puddings. The party were taken by police cars to a local prison to be kept overnight. The players were released the next day but too late to play in the match.

It was another blunder by Mr. Keighley that gave the gendarmes a lead to trace the receiver of the contraband goods. Each black pudding was stamped with a picture of goal posts and the word 'Long Live the Super League'. Immediately the gendamerie raided the offices of the Dieppe Onion and Garlic Co. The owner, Monsewer Chefsalleyway, ex rugby league international and onion grower, was caught in the act of packing brandy, perfume and nylons which he intended to trade for the black puddings. The two culprits are in prison awaiting trial. Monsewer Chefsalleyway is reputed to be the notorious 'Black Hand' who ran a very successful smuggling business before the war. Directors of his club said they now feared that he would be no longer involved in the proposed Super League. His partner, Septimus Scragbottom, is said to be very upset by the news. The gendarmes are perfectly satisfied that he had nothing to do with the smuggling."

Joshua folded the paper in front of a stunned Clara.
"...That's it, lass. He's put his size twelves in it reet this time. Make us a brew, Clara love. I reckon it's summat of a shock to us systems.

Sit down, first love. 'Appen he'll not get too badly treated."

"Silly ass! He's his own worst enemy is Stanley. Fancy him guessing the french onion man was a crook. Takes one to know one me old dad used to say. Will they decontaminate him on the gellatine?"

"Nay. That's all gone now. That went out with the Three Musketeers and all that stuff. He'll be put in jail I reckon."

"I've heard terrible tales about that Bastile place . . . they had to eat rats at one time. Mind you, he deserves it does the lad. 'Appen it'll bring him to his senses. I suppose he'll lose his job as scout now? And what will I do with the business? I'll have to get one of those locust undertakers in what take over when you're poorly. It'll drain all us money. Wait till I get him to meself, I'll give him what for!"

"As regards his scouting job, lass, we'll have to discuss it at meeting. Bob Kearsley's a bit prudish at times but I reckon as I'll talk him round. Besides in a funny way Stanley has done me a good turn."

"How come?" asked Clara mashing the tea on the hob.

"It'll be the end of the Super League. I know it breaks your heart, lass. You're a hard working woman like most of 'em in Northern towns, come up through t'mills and had to graft like heck. You're entitled to a bit of glamour, but I never reckoned as it would work, lass. It were killing me all that worry. I were made out to be a rogue and a vagabond – trust speccies to put me on t'rack. Quick to condemn are the speccies at all clubs – they're a funny lot. Any road, between me, you and our moggy I'm not sorry. Are you with me?"

"Ee, lad, I could kiss you! You're a Champion Chairman. Hang on while I put me top set in first, they come loose when I get upset."

"Don't bother, lass . . . . keep all your affection for that husband of yours, he'll not get much for a long while."

"He'll sleep in coffin shop when he gets back! That's the way to treat 'em . . . . Fancy, bungling the job! The big bake!"

"Oh! So you didn't mind him smuggling? It's not wrong then?"

This was a new angle. Typical woman, thought Joshua.

"Well, nylons and odour colognny perfume . . . I'd have been talk of the town and look what silly bugger did, made a balls of it!"

"Clara Keighley, what would vicar say!" Joshua was genuinely shocked.

Clara chose not to reply. Instead she knocked hell out of the aspidistra in the old art pot with a feather duster and muttered blood curdling threats to her incarcerated spouse.

Chapter 10

They say that hell hath no fury like a woman scorned. That is as maybe but what is certain is that a woman who loses out because of the stupidity of a man is a spectacle of anger to behold. When that anger is multiplied by three, uncontrolled fury would be the only term to fit the bill suitably. In that grimy old fashioned town of Bramfield nestling in the shade of the rugged Pennines a very unholy fury indeed was brewing in the hearts of three women stunted in their ambitions by an overweight undertaker of the name of Stanley Keighley.

Miss Hyacinth Grimshaw literally cried into her Crème de Menthe. She had been on the verge of creating history. The very first female administrator in rugby league, a position of pride and importance. To her the Super League would have been the ladder to a career woman's dream. The shock had turned her into a chain smoker. Sticking one Du Maurier after another into her ebony encrusted cigarette holder she inhaled the soothing smoke in an attempt to intoxicate her brain and soothe her nerves. Gladys Grimshaw, to give her the name she was baptised with, had been born in Gobstone Ginnel, a cobbled cut between Bagworthys Maggot Farm and Caseys Chemical Works. Gladys had always had ambitions to better herself and while other girls were playing hop scotch and skipping over ropes she was learning to speak correctly at an elocutionist, the lessons paid for out of her spending money. Sophisticated airs went hand in glove with her scholastic achievements, soon she was a leading member of the university thespians who all thought that she had been born in St. Albans. She had hoped for greater things than work as a mill secretary but Mr. Hepplethwaite was prepared to pay more money than she would have earned as a teacher. Surrounded by the harshness of Northern life her sensitive nature rebelled as she longed for the more refined life of a southern town like Winchester or Bath, and as for helping her employer run a rugby league club . . . well! What would her university chums have thought! Most had married union types. Serving in the land army, which was peopled mainly by girls of sensitivity, had inspired her to set her sights and aspirations on greater things which meant employment more in keeping with her social status. The Super League had been the answer. It would still be the sport of the working classes but the international aspect of the new set up appealed to her, she was a French speaker, her administrative skills had been applauded by the hierarchy at the Leeds H.Q. – and now due to 'that fool' Keighley her hopes and ambitions were in ashes at her feet.

"Ee, I could throttle bugger!" she screeched slipping back for a second to her native tongue. What a fool she had been not to realise he was in the Black Market long ago. Even the Du Mauriers she was smoking had come from him. If only she had realised and reported him to the authorities! To be thus thwarted was almost unbearable.

In the wash house Clara Keighley knocked hell out of the clothes in the dolly tub thrusting the dolly peg into them with an almost evil gusto pretending they were her bungling husband Stanley. What the vicar would have said I don't know, but the words she uttered were far removed from the text of a methodist prayer book. After the washing had been done she sat on the cobbles in the back yard and wept her heart out. Branded the wife of an international smuggler she was washed up as far as becoming a prominent lady of the town. She knew how the gossips in the small community would talk. It would all come out about her husband's Black Market activities during the war. Honest to goodness hard working people they wouldn't take kindly to folks eating off the fat of the land when everyone else was barely existing. She should have known it was too good to be true. There was as much chance of Stanley becoming a director as there was of Unos Dabs* winning the Rugby League Cup. Why the hell hadn't she listened to her dad! The vicar had pleaded with her not to wed Stanley, but with him being the Rovers scout she felt sort of flattered that he'd proposed. After all she'd been a Rovers fan since she could walk. "I don't care if he does have to eat rats in the Bastion place, it'll larn him. I wed a reet balm pot in yon mon. Me dad always said he didn't know if he were on this earth or fullers – a yed full o'jolly robins as me mam used to say."

On the other side of the town a doomed silence reigned in Joshua Hepplethwaite's abode. His wife's reaction to the abandoning of the Super League was to go into a deep sulk. This brown study lasted fully two days. Joshua was sick to death of washing up and cooking but what annoyed him most of all was that he was being blamed along with Stanley. Such is the strange reasoning of women folk she couldn't (or wouldn't) separate her husband's part in the Super League materialisation from that of Stanley's wrong doing. The silence at last gave way to a fit of pique in which she lambasted Joshua verbally. When the anger was spent the last words Joshua heard were "...So much for me ruddy Paris hat!", which were uttered in a despairing whisper.

If Stanley Keighley could have felt the boiling anger of these
* *St. Helens Amatuer R.L. Team*

three thwarted women he would have died of acute shame. Not only had he disgraced the English Rugby League but he would be branded as a cad and a rotter. But all that was worrying Stanley was the thought that all the burial work in the town would go to Horace Holroyd and someone else would get his scouting job. Holroyds were offering two burials for the price of one already.

As for Joshua, well Stan had got him into lumber before and probably would do so again. He would never admit it of course but he was relieved. In his heart of hearts he knew he wasn't the Super League type. Neither was Bramfield a Super League town. For that matter neither were Batley, Dewsbury and the rest of the Northern towns. All folks wanted was to get back to normal after the war, the old traditional way of going on would do them for a long time to come. There was a lightness in his step, a song in his heart, as he walked to the mill down mucky back entries and grim cobbled back alleys. The knocker-up on the way home from his early morning stint raising the sleepy work force; the paper lad in flat cap and braces; old Ma Murgatroyd white stoning the front door step; the stink of the stagnant canal as it blended with the stench of boiled bones from the knacker's yard; the friendly "Ow do, Josh lad" from the driver of the midden wagon – familiar sounds, familiar sights. Ee by gum, they sounded and looked reet grand! Lancashire wasn't going to change.

The league supporters in both counties were agog with the news of the failure of the new league. Ninety per cent were delighted. Like it or not Stanley was turning into a sort of folk hero along the lines of Jesse James and the Wild Colonial Boy. Outside the town hall in St. Helens they were dancing in the square. The thought of joining up with Wigan had given people sleepless nights. After years of yelling for Ken Gees blood the last thing they wanted to do was to applaud him when he played for Wigan St. Helens. What a bloody mess it would have been! With top class centres like Ted Ward and Ernie Ashcroft of Wigan and Jimmy Stott of Saints who the hell was going to stand down? It would have been a shambles.

The feelings of Saints followers were echoed by the supporters of the other clubs forced to amalgamate.

From Bramley to Broughton, from Leeds to Barrow, relief at the cancellation of the Super League was made apparent by the joyous reaction in pubs and clubs. At the headquarters in Leeds however it was a different story. The press bombarded the top brass officials with awkward questions and the name Stanley Keighley was almost guaranteed to make them explode into a stream of invectives. In a nutshell they were extremely embarrassed.

Joshua was off the hook. Twice nightly variety was opening up again at the Hippodrome after it had been used as a recruiting centre and a British restaurant during the war. Ee . . . . it were reet exciting. Him and Pheobe Maud would book a box every week just like they'd done before the war. Some great acts had been booked – Stanelli and his Hornchestra, Dawsons Canaries, Wilson, Kepple and Betty, the sand dancers, Harry Mooney and Victor King, Albert Butters performing mice, Jimmy O'Dea and Company from Dublin . . . Ee . . . what a treat! Life was looking up and such was the joy in Joshuas heart that he burst into song as he took a short cut through Brogdens bone yard to the mill:

Mister Izzy Rubenstein who was very old one day when playing tiddly winks caught a nasty cold, his great, great grandson wrapped him up and put him into bed. His lawyer called next morning and this is what he said:

"Is Mister Izzy ill? Is he? Is He?
Has he caught a chill? Has he? Has he?
The slightest cold often turns to flu
Appendicitis, Tonsillitis and Bronchitis too – – –
Is he breathing still? Is he? Is he?
Will he make a will? Will he? Will he?
I am Izzys lawyer and I've called around because I want to know
is Izzy worse or is he has he was?

No one tried to answer him much to his dismay. The lawyers face
went very white as he was heard to say:

Now I've had charge of his affairs since 1862
He owes me six and eight pence so tell me quickly do:
Is Mister Izzy ill? Is he? Is he?
Has he caught a chill? Has he? Has he?
The slightest cold often turns to 'flu
Appendicitis, Tonsillitus and Bronkitikus too
Will he make a will? Will he? Will he?
I am Izzys lawyer and I've called around because
I want to know is Izzy worse or is he has he was?"

He even did a little dance and spun his hard hat in the air as he
dodged the globules of filth that floated on the slight breeze. It was
a mucky town but he felt reet glad to be in it that morning. By gum
he did 'an all!

"Lummy Mr. Hepplethwaite it's fair fettled the cockles of me
heart to hear you singing." It was Sam Smallbottom the local rat
catcher, "I want to shake your hand and wish Rovers all the best for
the new season."

But Joshuas happy mood was sullied by the expression on his
secretary's face. It was enough to turn ale sour. The last thing he
wanted was another woman in a bad mood. Hyacinth gave him a
look that would have withered a Yorkshire scrum half. "Carrying
t'can" he said to himself. "Sod it" he thought "They'll get over it."

"There's a very important letter for you, Mr. Hepplethwaite. I
suggest you give it your urgent attention". He could almost detect
a sense of glee in his secretary's tone which immediately irritated
him. She's getting too big for her boots is the wench were his
thoughts.

"I'm not bloody having it!" Snatching the letter he scanned it
eagerly.

Dear Sir,

As the Chairman of Bramfield Rover RLFC we hold you personally responsible for the disgraceful affair in France involving your scout Mr. S. Keighley. Such despicable behaviour brings the game into disrepute and has been partially responsible for the abandonment of the Super League. You are called to attend an urgent meeting on Thursday next to discuss the implications of this incident. Your failure to do so will result in the immediate closure of your club.
Yours faithfully
Jonah Hawksbody
Sec. to R.L.F.C. Leeds H.Q.

Much to Miss Grimshaw's surprise and disappointment her employer only guffawed appearing to be not in the least upset by the letter.

"Well, what are you staring at lass? Get thee pen and do summat for thee living. Lets get fettling. I don't pay thee good brass to gawp wench."

This unaccustomed outburst had the desired affect. Within seconds Hyacinth was once again the devoted secretary.

"Take this letter down: *Dear Mr. Hawksbody, I am in receipt of your letter and note its contents. I shall not be attending the meeting at Leeds so whatever decision you reach can be forwarded to me. I enclose a photograph taken at a Paris Night Club, I trust you enjoyed yourself. I have several copies of same which will be distributed if necessary. Yours truly Joshua Hepplethwaite, Chairman, Bramfield Rover R.L.F.C.*

As Joshua had anticipated the letter and the photograph did the trick.

The new season opened in late August and as the players ran onto the field the crowd were agog with excitement over the lettering on the Rovers' strip.

"Foggs for Ferrets" was emblazoned on front and back. Joshua had negotiated the very first sponsorship in Rugby League. When Jimmy Bott kicked off for the Rovers the crowd roared. Not for a very long time had the Rovers directors felt such a thrill. All the bottled up excitement of the speccies was let loose in that roar. Bramfield V. Bruddersby! By tradition the opening match of the season. "Come on lads, get 'em fettled!" shouted Joshua rising to his feet in the director's box. Bob Kearsley handed him the club pickle jar. "Appen we'll be able to afford a new jar with t'sponsorship brass, Josh?"

"Aye, 'appen we will" said Joshua stabbing a large one with his pickle tooth. "It's better than eating bloody frogs legs, any road!"

"Get stuck in you nesh bugger!" shouted old Ma Muckberry aged eighty nine and still as active with her tongue as ever.

"Tackle him don't bloody kiss him!" she roared, stabbing her umbrella in fury as the Bruddersby right wing ran through his opponent.

"No wonder they call em the easy six!" Roared an irate Yorkshire miner still in his pit black as the Rovers scrum half wriggled his way through the Bruddersby pack to score.

"I wouldn't pay 'em with washers! Get the bugger fettled he's nobbut a babby!"

"Put ref. a jersey on! Have you lost thee pee ref?"

"Ast got a white stick ref.?" All the stock rugby league insults were being hurled about. One of the Bruddersby supporters was getting very fed up with the banter from the Rovers crowds and his verbal retaliation was cruel in the extreme and aimed at Dolly Broadbottom the Rovers hooker who had just stiff armed an opponent who needed the magic sponge..

'Dolly' was no oil painting. Cauliflower ears, a broken nose, no teeth, he was a typical hard as nails bullocking 'forrard' of the period.

"Look at yon mon the ugly sod!" Shouted the Yorkshire man.

"His mug makes a monkeys backside look like Kew Gardens!"
Even the Rovers speccies joined in the laughter. All the traditional
banter heard through the years on every ground was being trundled
out. War time rugby was over; it was back to the serious stuff again.
Although the supporters of both teams pretended to hate each other
not one blow was made in anger.

Up in the best stand, the directors were lapping up the atmosphere.

"Ee its good to be back to normal Joshua" said Hadfield
Barnacre seriously. "Listening to all the old banter, its like sweet
music to us ears." For once Joshua agreed with his hated rival.
"Aye, it is and all Hadfield owd sprout. And not a bloody French
man in sight!"

The two rivals grinned and shook hands.

Ee, it were reet grand to be normal again!